FROM A ͟G PRINCESS

Heal from heartbreak and magically manifest true love

Author and Illustrator: Nazish S. Qazi

Lessons from a Frog Princess

Copyright © 2022: Nazish S. Qazi

All rights reserved. No part of this publication may be produced, distributed, or transmitted in any form or by any means, including photocopying, recording, or other electronic or mechanical methods, without the prior written permission of the publisher, except in the case of brief quotations embodied in critical reviews and certain other non-commercial uses permitted by copyright law.

This book is for general information purposes and nothing contained in it is, or is intended to be construed as advice. It does not take into account your individual health, medical, physical or emotional situation or needs. It is not a substitute for medical attention, treatment, examination, advice, treatment of existing conditions or diagnosis and is not intended to provide a clinical diagnosis nor take the place of proper medical advice from a fully qualified medical practitioner.

First Printed in United Kingdom 2022

Published by Conscious Dreams Publishing
www.consciousdreamspublishing.com

Edited by Elise Abram

Illustrations by Nazish S. Qazi

Cover design by Andreas Klein

Typeset by Oksana Kosovan

ISBN: 978-1-913674-88-5

This book is dedicated to
mí maravilloso compañero a del alma, mein Froschkönig

Contents

Testimonials 7

1. First Flame 11
   Falling Frogling 12
   Love's Tough Training 15
   About the Book 17
   The Lessons 19

2. Faking the Fairy tale 25
   Down the Rabbit Hole 26
   Gasping for Life 30
   To Begin Again 34

3. Rivers of Release 43
   The Toad Prince 44
   River of Tears 48
   The Grieving Process 51

4. Sitting on a Rock 59
   Bon Voyage 60
   Making Me Time 62
   Facing Facts 64
   Going Inside 67

5. The Princess Awakens 77
   Becoming a Princess 78
   Genuine Freedom 82
   Most Valuable Treasure 87

6. Tuning into Magic 99
   Peter Pan 100
   A New Direction 104
   Fairy Godmother 109
   Summon the Genie 112

7. The Dragon's Lair...129
- Another Frog..130
- Facing the Truth...134
- The Buried Past..140
- Meeting My Dragon...144

8. Breaking the Curse...161
- A True Prince...162
- Treasure Chests..167
- Unchaining Myself...175
- Forgiveness...177

9. Weaving a Magic Spell...189
- Mr Not Right...190
- Mr Fantastic...193
- Trove of Treasures..199
- Ticket to the Ball...213

10. An Enchanted Island...221
- Dancing Feet..222
- An Extraordinary Prediction...233
- How Manifestation Works..242
- Coming Home..263

About the Author...267

Acknowledgements..269

References..273

Testimonials

"A few years ago, I was extremely lucky to meet Nazish who introduced me to this beautiful method for changing my mindset and my life as a result.

At the time, when I first started to use it, I was going through some great changes on my life's path. I had to make a big decision about my future and sometimes, I felt that I was missing the right person next to me to support me at such important moments.

Then, I used this approach, not just for my work life but for my love life as well. How surprised I was when I decided move to a different country for my work and on the same day, my boyfriend and I met! I knew we were truly meant for each other and supposed to meet at that point in our lives. We have been very happy together ever since.

It truly felt like I was in a fairy tale when everything was coming together, just like magic in my life!!"

– **AG**

* * *

"Hi Nazish, I wanted to tell you that I found the love of my life! And it *is* possible, thanks to your work. I was just reviewing the exercises you showed me one year ago, of writing about what I want, and my new partner has got all of that and much more! WOW!!

Even more so, it helped me to integrate these positives in myself, too. I was very open to receiving your help to change my old tendency of having pain in my relationships and you made it happen. The way you coached me and how gentle you were, touching my 'negative dragons', really helped me to heal that part of my life. So, I feel very blessed with him, my life is completely different now and more authentic, and that is because of you, too.

Great job, Nazish, brilliant! Really valuable coaching."

– AMV

* * *

"When I first met Nazish, I wasn't doing so well. I had been single for many years and looking for the right partner without any success. So I started the coaching and we worked on my confidence using various *interesting* techniques. At first, I was sceptical about whether it would help at all, but I soon learned better. Only a few weeks after doing that special exercise, I found my perfect, loving partner. He just walked into my life without my even trying! Today, we are still very happy together, even after many years."

– LS

* * *

"Nazish is an amazing coach. I benefitted from her work back in 2012 when I was going through some personal turmoil in my life. She introduced me to some simple mind exercises, journal writing and how to manifest the things I want. Life since then has been amazing, including finding true love, my Mr Right, and I still continue to practice all that I learned."

– SA

* * *

"Dear Nazish, I can hardly believe it... but I am SO happy that I have met my wonderful partner for life! Really! I'm still breathless, speechless and blown away. A man came into my life some weeks ago, and the past few days with him were like a dream... All I can say is WOW! Your magic really works." (2016)

"Now, five years later, it has touched me deeply to read what I wrote again. After all this time, those words are still valid and I am very grateful for the incredible magic I got to experience through having worked with you. The magic is still present every day in my life in every relationship, with my partner, family, friends and ultimately, with myself. I sincerely thank you from the bottom of my heart for your wonderful mentorship." (2021)

– AH

* * *

"After using the freedom technique – this magic – I can tell you that I felt as though, for the first time in MANY years, that I was free, in every sense of the word. It was a gentle release, as if I'd just taken flight with wings that I didn't know I had! It's incredible but I can, hand on heart, reassure you that this method really works. For the first time in 12 years, I had a co-parenting conversation with my son's father! Yup. And since, I have continued to experience more peaceful conversations and interactions that previously, would never have happened! Or if they had, would have left me emotionally drained for days. I now keep this technique in my 'harmony wellbeing' toolkit."

– VH

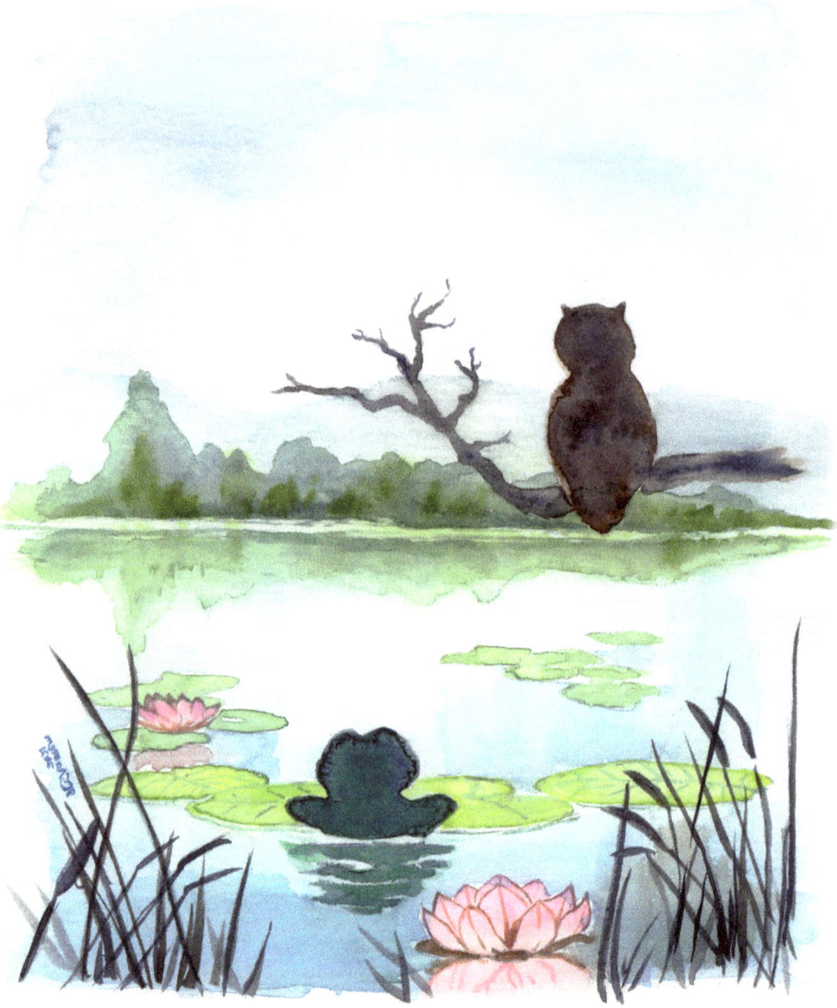

1. First Flame

Out there, in the middle of the pond, amidst the cool, deep waters, the tastiest of treats were to be found. But only the most charming and handsome of creatures were permitted to partake of that reserve. Alas, little froglings were not invited for they must hide in the grassy shallows, along the muddy banks.

There she would sit, waiting for a tiny morsel to fly her way, hoping that she herself might not become a morsel, too.

"If I cannot see how I look –," she peered into the murkiness but found no reflection, "how shall I ever know who I am?" she pondered sadly. "Well, I suppose it matters not for no one notices me anyway."

Yet, in her heart, she nurtured a secret dream; to swim amongst the chosen ones and taste those forbidden treats. And that one day, she might venture even farther... and beyond.

Falling Frogling

"Where is he?" I mumbled to myself, straining to look through the crowds. "Oh, do get out of the way!" I mentally urged them to move out of my line of vision. Along with the hundreds of other teenagers, I stood outside, huddled together with my friends, watching the boys kick a football about. It was break time at school on a cold October day as we stood on the tarmac playgrounds which were otherwise used as netball or tennis courts. We chatted, hunching our shoulders and shuffling our feet, trying to keep warm. I tried to join in with the conversation but my mind was preoccupied, as usual. Surreptitiously, my eyes flitted over towards the farthest playground where my heart lay.

As a child, I was rather quiet as my English was poor and so, I grew up being the outsider, the odd one in class. By the time I had reached secondary school, I was a fully-fledged nerd. By 'nerd', I mean one of the old-fashioned variety – not the smart, clever, bespectacled whiz kids of today. Nerd status meant being designated to the 'B' group, or sometimes the 'C' group, which consisted of all the awkward, weird, shy, uncool kids that I affectionately like to call 'froglings'. Of course, these 'B' and 'C' groups were not to be confused with our academic abilities. These were determined by the unspoken and unfair, yet perfectly understood, rules of social groups that teenagers naturally form in every generation.

The much cooler 'A' group would avoid hanging around us or sitting next to us in class. Worst of all would be when they had to choose one of us as a partner in 'PE'. And as for romance, the boys would never cast a second glance at a frogling like me. Being ugly, quiet, not very clever and the only Asian, brown-skinned girl in my year meant that I would never qualify as girlfriend material. I don't know if they were actually being prejudiced. Most probably, because I was different, they simply didn't quite know how to relate to me.

Yet, this frogling dreamed of her happy-ever-after fairy tale. She was most content when drifting off into her own imaginary world of some sweet, innocent, romantic story about one Prince Charming or another. When suddenly, one fine morning, something happened that would send her on a long, long journey, out of her daydreams and into the real world of love... and loss.

Despite being a thirteen-year-old frogling in my unfashionable, out-of-date charity shop clothes and dull, flat hair, it never occurred to me that I didn't stand a chance with one of the coolest guys in school. I was completely smitten with Mark. He was tall, broad, very good looking and in the 'A' group. He had twinkling eyes, a cheeky smile and smoked cigarettes – so grown up! (In those days, shopkeepers didn't check IDs before selling cigarettes.) He was everything my naïve mind had imagined a smart, swarthy young man should be.

Although we were in the same year, I would never see Mark during classes. He was in a different group of classes and my only chance would be at break and lunch times. Since noticing him in the lunch queue at the beginning of term, I couldn't get him out of my mind. "One day, he is going to notice me too, and of course, we will fall madly in love with each other..." I thought, day dreaming happily.

But on that particular morning, everything changed. That break time was different. As usual, I peered across the playgrounds towards the far corner where I knew he would be hanging around with his friends. Eventually, a little window cleared through the crowds, just enough for me to catch a glimpse of my heart's desire.

"Ah, there you are," I thought as my heart lifted and then, instantly dropped. Mark was sitting on the ground as he often did, with his long legs stretched out in front of him, having a smoke. But now, there was a *girl* sitting on his lap! She had short brown hair and it looked as though she was wearing *his* jacket! They were chatting and laughing together as he warmed her hands in his. Then he took the cigarette out of his mouth and placed it to her lips.

For a second, I was confused. I stood rigid, eyes wide, trying to take in the scene. As comprehension washed over me, my heart started to pound, my breath stopped. It was as though a sledgehammer had hit me. I felt stunned! A moment later, I turned away and was running. Running from my friends. Running and pushing through the crowds. Tears streaming down my face, my insides turning upside down. I ran and ran.

No one cared or seemed to notice me disappear. I glanced over my shoulder one more time and caught sight of the two of them, now kissing. "NO! No, no!" I wanted the ground to open up and swallow me. "How could you be so stupid?" I scolded myself. Until then, it had never crossed my mind, not once, that my dream might get broken, that my sweet, happy-ever-after story could go so very wrong! Nothing had ever prepared me for such a possibility.

Finally, I stopped running and leaned against the back wall of the library, my head spinning, my stomach wrenching. I needed to be alone, to not think and not feel, but I couldn't stop the stinging, agonising sobs spilling out.

After a while, the bell rang and break time was over. Time to head to the next class. My two friends found me shaking and battling tears. I didn't need to explain. They too, had seen Mark with that girl and knew exactly what must have happened to me. They tried their best to console and comfort me.

"How silly are you? What were you thinking?!" I continued to berate myself over and over. "Never, ever again!"

When, at last, the shock was over, I decided that I would never be such a fool again and allow myself to fall so blindly for a boy. This was my first lesson in how unfair love could be and so, I learnt that I should be more realistic about my expectations. "Before jumping in, I must always consider every possibility and not just give my heart away so easily," I promised myself. "The next time, for sure, I *will* choose the right one."

Love's Tough Training

Thus, the long and arduous journey of my romantic life began with the first of many fairy tale dreams being smashed. Of course, it was just a typical teenage crush, you might say. A case of simple infatuation, but at the time, it felt like real love. I remember being completely and utterly besotted with Mark. Unrequited love, no matter what the age, is still heart-achingly painful. However long, short or fleeting a relationship might be, nothing ever really prepares us for having our hearts broken. All we can do is accept that there will be such agonies in life and try to learn from them. It might also have helped had I been a little more cautious and prudent in my choice to begin with.

I remember desperately wishing, "If only I had a magic wand that could change his feelings and make him like me. Or at least, something to stop me from liking him so I could be spared making such an idiot of myself". Of course, being only thirteen and incredibly naïve, I had absolutely no idea about boys or relationships. My poor young heart lay broken but there was no one to turn to and so, I learned to push down the pain.

Many years later, I realised I might never have had any interest in Mark at all, if I had acquired even a modicum of self-worth. But I had none. No self-understanding, self-esteem or self-confidence, whatsoever. I had received no education about matters of the heart and was never given any such guidance. If I had been taught anything about real life or had at least a little self-respect, then perhaps, I might have been less hungry to begin with and not so hurt when someone like him didn't notice me.

I still find it curious that despite having had so many teachers, parents and various respected elders around as I was growing up, none were able to teach me any useful lessons about love. Neither did I find any guidance in books, journals or documentaries during those formative years. On the contrary, I only learned from my role models how to be bad at relationships and marriage.

Being a nerd, I would spend many contented hours in the library. I pored through books on psychology but found nothing that explained how to have a good, healthy and happy relationship. Other than my own endless determination to find true love, I had little else to guide me. Except, of course, for the great wisdom I gleaned from teenage girls' magazines and romance novels! Unwittingly, as I happily soaked up the drama of Hollywood and Bollywood movies, the foundations of my romantic life were being cast.

It seemed that despite the 'love crazed cultures' we live in, there was little in the way of useful education available to prepare a young person for one of life's most important ventures. Hence, I learned the hard way, through stumbling, struggling and standing up again, and again, by myself. Over the next three decades, I acquired a volume of knowledge about relationships through finding, falling and failing in love.

As the frogling hopped into adulthood, she became very aware of her frogginess and worked hard to grow into a worthy princess. She soon discovered the easy path, and much later, the less travelled path to princesshood. Along the way, she met many frogs. Some turned out to be toads and some genuine princes, but alas, none that could truly fit the shoe. Every time she fell deep into the pond of love, she would inevitably, find herself in yet another quagmire of disappointment and despondence. However, all is not lost, for on this journey, she gathered a wealth of valuable lessons and discovered the hidden treasures that lead to authentic, genuine love.

About the Book

This book is therefore, written with the intention of helping those who have loved and lost, as a guide to overcoming heartache and finding a truly fulfilling relationship. It offers much more than suggestions for developing your self-worth and self-love practices. Here, you will take a journey, step-by-step, through learning exactly how to release all the sorrow, sadness and agony in order to mend your broken heart and heal the past. First, I will help you clear any past baggage that you may still unconsciously be holding onto and change the psychological programmes of repeating old patterns.

Secondly, I will show you how to delve into your extraordinary brain to unlock the hidden barriers and create a new reality, one that you truly deserve. You will learn some amazing secret skills in how to magically manifest your own beautiful fairy tale. Once you learn to harness this ability, you will also find the answers to your long-held questions, the lessons behind those tough life experiences and gain a much deeper knowledge of yourself and your heart's true direction.

The purpose of this book is perfectly summarised by some very wise advice from my dear mother:

> *"If someone brought you a gift, something that you really like, perhaps a bag of delicious fresh fruit or sweet treats, what kind of dish would you choose to receive them in? Would you get a plate that's already filled with yesterday's leftovers or an empty one? And would you put them on a plate that is dirty and unwashed? Would you find a tiny bowl that is too small? Well, of course not. You would find a nice dish, which has been properly cleared and cleaned. And you would make sure that it is the appropriate size and shape to hold this delicious gift, right?*
>
> *Therefore, it is the same in life. If you want to receive all the good, delicious things that life wants to offer you, you must first make sure your dish is cleared, cleaned and big enough."*

This book will help you do precisely that; clear your heart, make space and align yourself to receive your soul's desire. You will then open a path to attracting the right kind of loving relationship and become a magnet for the one you truly deserve. I sincerely hope that you don't have to go through as many years of longing, loneliness and heartache, as I did. Once you have read and completed the exercises in this book, I feel confident that you won't have to wait too long before your Mr or Ms Right walks into your life.

To help you better understand how 'The Lessons' came to be, I have shared some accounts from my personal life. These are very private experiences which, until today, have remained firmly locked away in a trunk, deep in the archives of my memory banks. I used to think that I would never utter a word about these secret stories because I was raised to believe that it is shameful to have more than one life partner. However, real life is not so straight forward and, as I have learned so much from those previous relationships, I feel it pertinent to share them with you. I hope that these good and bad experiences can help you make sense of yours.

Please note: all the names of individuals mentioned in the stories have been changed in order to protect their privacy.

The Lessons

So, exactly how do you go about healing a broken heart? What happens now that your relationship is definitely over? Other than a few close friends to lean on, perhaps you feel quite empty or lost? What if it has been months or even years since your last relationship and you still find yourself being plagued with the agony of your ex? Or perhaps, you feel your heart has completely mended and you are now ready to find the elusive Mr/Ms Right? The only problem is you worry that you might attract someone like your ex again and you really couldn't stand to go through another heartbreak.

In The Lessons sections, you will find exercises to help you answer these questions. By using these tools you will know exactly what you need to learn, do and practise. They include practical, written and meditative exercises, which are mostly about 'thinking', and less 'doing', type of tasks. Simply follow the straightforward, step-by-step instructions at a time and pace to suit you.

For the exercises, you will need:

- 2 x small/medium-sized paper notebooks, pens and a pencil
- sticky notes/Post-it Notes
- a voice recorder such as a mobile phone App or other device
- pair of earphones

In some of the exercises, I will ask you to make written notes on paper. You may be tempted to write everything using a digital device such as your computer, mobile phone, tablet or similar gadget. However, I strongly recommend that you write by hand and on paper. Research has shown that the process of writing by hand activates the parts of your brain that help you store and learn more effectively than typing onto a device.[1]

Before you learn the new skills for manifestation, you will need to 'unlearn' some outdated thought programmes, then reframe and heal from them. This is the purpose of the meditative visualisations which are designed to transform your subconscious thinking processes. These are very powerful tools so do not miss any of the steps and please follow the detailed instructions precisely.

I will hold your hand and help you through the whole process. All you need to do is trust the way The Lessons work and accept that *you can* do this. This is why you are here and have chosen to read this book. Start now by affirming this intention in your mind, "I am easily healing, growing and learning. I am manifesting all that I need and desire to be happy."

This is not just another nice 'how-to' book with theoretical self-improvement ideas and suggestions; it is much more. This is a life coach telling you *exactly* how to get yourself from where you are now, to where you want to be, using no-nonsense language and clear guidance. Your dream does not need to remain a fantasy forever if you have a sincere desire not to let your past dictate your future and are willing to put in the effort and 'self-work'. Don't worry – there is nothing too complicated or tough to do but it will need your time and patience to make the changes happen, from the inside out.

As you read the stories, you will find they are not in chronological order but recounted so that they correspond with The Lessons given in each chapter. This is to help you learn progressively and develop your abilities in a way that will be most effective and beneficial for your healing. Therefore, I suggest that when you read this book for the first time, do *not* to skip or skim any of the pages. Take your time to read through the chapters and do the exercises sequentially, in the order given.

Once you have completed all the exercises, you can go back and use it as a reference book or jump to relevant chapters or exercises as and when you need. As you become more practised, you can adapt some of the exercises accordingly. However, in the first instance, especially if you are completely new to this kind of self-work, it is best to follow the directions closely.

Before we begin, please note these important points:

- You are about to make some big life changes. These are not temporary changes and should not be taken light-heartedly.
- Be kind to yourself as you take a leap into unknown territory. It is okay to feel a little hesitant or anxious at first. Just trust that this is a healing and learning process and that by the end, you will become a much better version of yourself.

- The Lessons hold the secret to some very powerful techniques for manifestation. You may learn and master these tools for good and beneficial purposes only; for yourself and others you care about. These tools cannot be used for any kind of negative purpose and do not work if your intention is to cause anyone harm. On the contrary, if you harbour any such ideas, you will only manifest negativity and harm upon yourself. It is, therefore, wiser to focus your time and energy on positive outcomes for your own healing, health and happiness.

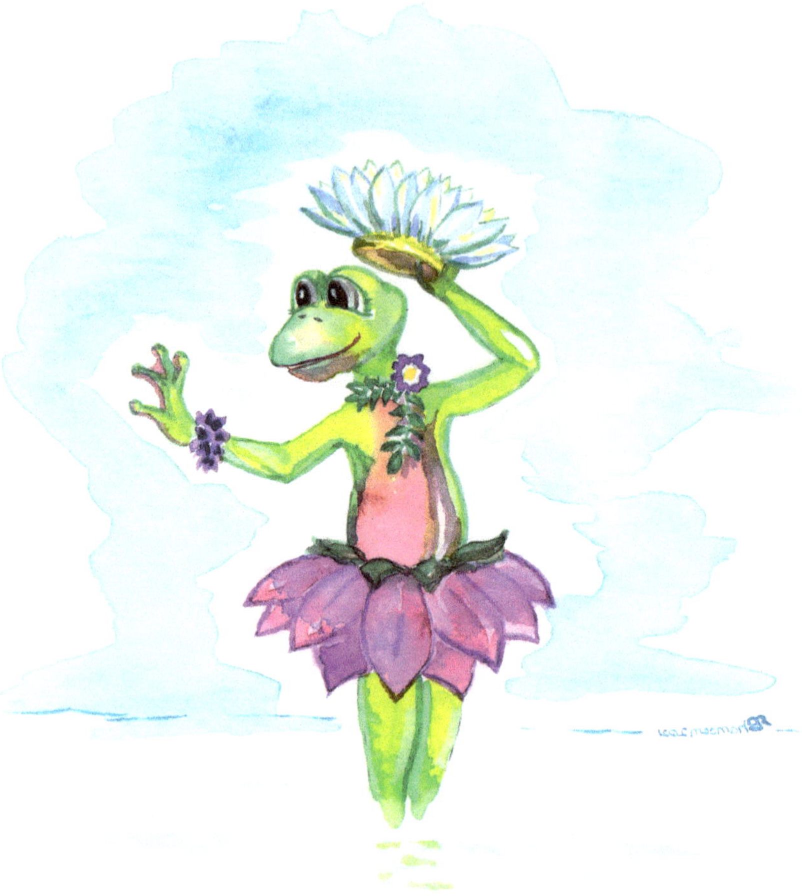

2. Faking the Fairy tale

"Oh, look at me! Am I not beautiful in all my finery?" she cooed, twirling in front of the mirror.
"Indeed, you are. But, dear princess, are you truly happy?" asked the mirror, quite concerned.
"Well, what an absurd question! Of course, I am happy. I have all that a young princess could ever wish for," she answered, rather haughtily. "I have gorgeous gowns, gold and gems and so many pretty shoes! I even have this ivory tower and my very own carriage. And of course, I have a handsome prince to marry me."
"But is he the gallant knight of your true desires?" asked the mirror. The princess sniffed but didn't answer.
"What do you know? You're only a mirror," she thought.

Down the Rabbit Hole

It was a cold, grey afternoon, mid-December, 1992. Outside, the sky was already growing dark as night began to draw in. I sat on the bed in my old bedroom, looking down at my beautifully hennaed hands which were decorated by my beloved sister. Dozens of thin, red and gold coloured glass bangles adorned my wrists. My neck and ears lay heavy with the weight of Indian gold necklaces and earrings.

The gorgeously woven scarlet and gold silk *sari* had been perfectly pleated and wrapped around my small frame by my talented sister-in-law. My hair was pulled back into a small, elegant bun and draped with a *'shaal'* that matched my sari. I had done my own make-up and hair, making sure it was fairly traditional and not too glamorous. As my fingers toyed with the two thick gold bangles, I sat alone, anxiously waiting.

The ceremony would begin at four o'clock. I looked at my watch, but of course, as expected, everything was running late. My stomach churned with nerves, excitement and some other emotions which I couldn't quite figure out. I caught my breath as my eyes fell upon my own reflection in the mirror. Despite the weight of the heavy sari and jewellery, I looked the epitome of a beautiful traditional Bangladeshi bride, – like in those old Indian movies – just as I had always imagined and wished for.

It was not an arranged marriage. Ted and I had been secretly seeing each other for the past two years. But this *marriage* was not exactly what I had in mind. Not now, not like this, anyway. Apart from the one new set sent by my uncle, all the gold jewellery had been borrowed from my mother's collection. Only the sari and the two thick gold bangles were new, which she had bought for me. "The clothes and jewellery are always given by the groom's family. It's not supposed to be this way," I thought, disappointedly. "He couldn't even buy the ring." To save face,

I had bought a cheap one from a catalogue shop, because in the end, Ted couldn't afford it and he would need a wedding ring to put on my finger at the ceremony.

"This is supposed to be the happiest day of your life, right?" I thought, gloomily. "So, is this what you've grown up dreaming about your whole life; a pitiful little ceremony in the living room of your parent's house?" Earlier that morning, my father had given me a very sad look as he watched me running around, tidying up and putting up a few measly tinsel decorations in our living room. The bride-to-be was not supposed to be doing such jobs on her wedding day but getting pampered and treated like a princess.

"Money isn't everything," I reassured myself. "Anyway, didn't my mother do the same when she got married?" My father's family had very little money since the war, despite their middle-class heritage. In order to preserve their honour, my mother had bought her own wedding trousseau with all the necessary saris and gold and, unbeknownst to my father, had it sent to her own family's home. "That's what you do in a marriage. You give and take. Yes, I know Ted hasn't got a proper job yet, and we've had our ups and downs, but who hasn't? It will all be all right once we're married and living together," I said to myself, trying to bolster my flagging confidence.

"In the eyes of Allah, it is sinful! You can't do that!" my mother had exclaimed. "You are not an English girl and that is not allowed in our society!" She was outraged after I had disclosed my secret about Ted and that we just wanted to live together. Some days later, after she had calmed down, she said, "Well, why don't you just have a small *'Akht'* ceremony? Then you can live together freely, as husband and wife. If you're planning on getting married eventually, just take your vows now instead of later. Then, in a few years' time, when you're ready, you can have a proper big wedding, an English wedding." My mother was a formidable woman and I was not equipped to argue with her. She went ahead and made all the arrangements. And so, the Imam, an Islamic preacher, was booked and would come to our house to conduct the ceremonies.

So, here I am, having allowed myself to be persuaded into this *marriage* ceremony. First, however, we would require another pre-ceremony for my husband-to-be. He would have to convert to Islam and take an oath, accepting it as his main faith. "This is an absolute necessity", the Imam had instructed my mother.

This was followed by several difficult discussions and arguments with the very British Ted – a non-religious man – who could not accept why he should take such an oath. Especially since his parents, who were mildly Christian, were understandably, not at all happy about it. Many years later, I discovered that Ted did not need to change his religion at all. We could have gone ahead with the *Akht* without the oath taking part.

I watched through the bedroom window as Ted and his family arrived. My heart sank when I saw the anxious expression on his face. "He must be feeling even more stressed than me," I thought, pacing around the bedroom. Alas, poor Ted nervously went through it all by himself in the guestroom downstairs, whilst I had to wait upstairs. "Oh, just be grateful your parents agreed to let you be with him," I reassured myself, wishing the day would be over soon.

"Just a few people," my mother had promised but then she proceeded to tell all and sundry that her daughter was getting married. Now, some of my father's associates and irrelevant neighbours were all there, crowded into the living room, along with both of our families and best friends.

Finally, it was time. Traditionally, the women prepare the bride and bring her through to where the ceremony takes place and so, my younger sister and sister-in-law came up to fetch me. They smiled uneasily at me, sensing my emotions, fussing over my sari and hair and making sure everything was looking perfect. Then, with one in front taking my arm and the other behind me holding up my sari up, the three of us slowly descended the winding stairs.

With each step down, I distinctly remember feeling more apprehensive. Halfway down the stairs, something made me stop. I pretended to fiddle with my sari as if it were catching on my shoe when suddenly, a voice came up from nowhere and shouted in my head, "Run!" It wasn't actually a voice but rather a wave of *feeling* that rose up from somewhere down in the pit of my belly.

"No, of course, not! Don't be silly!" I thought, immediately brushing it off. "That's just nerves," I told myself and continued slowly down the stairs. "It is far too late now. You've made your commitments and you better keep them. There's a room full of people sitting, waiting for you. You can't just let them down! And anyway, aren't you getting just what you wanted? Marrying the guy *you* chose?" I admonished myself sternly and quickly pushed aside the nervous thoughts.

At the time, I had no idea that what I had heard – or rather, felt – was my inner voice, my 'gut feeling' crying out to me. I simply didn't know how to react to that intuitive warning and so, I did the best I could with what little knowledge I had at the time. We carried on down the stairs, continued as planned and went ahead with the ceremony. This marriage would be my chance to break free of the limitations and restrictions that had constrained me my whole life. So I was not about to let some silly nerves get in the way. No, I was not going to be held back anymore and I desperately needed to stretch my wings.

Gasping for Life

Over the years, the frogling worked hard and shed many of her old skins in order to become a fairly smart and capable princess. She believed that relationships, like everything in life, required a lot of hard work and effort to create a happy-ever-after fairy tale. "Surely, if I kiss him and love him enough, I will persevere," she thought, hoping her frog would eventually turn into a prince. Little did she know, that by walking into the bewitched idyll of marriage and ignoring her fairy godmother's warning, she was about to roll down the rabbit hole of no return. Her journey would lead to long, lonesome wanderings through caverns of gloom, defeating nasty dragons and conquering dark spells before she would find the real treasure her heart sought.

Many months later, early one Sunday morning, I found myself gasping for air and struggling to breathe. I had been lying awake the whole night with the most dreadful cough constricting my throat, causing me to wheeze from the depths of my lungs. I thought I was dying! The cough grew steadily worse and I was bewildered, not knowing what was happening to me or whom I could turn to. Ted had gone away that weekend for a gig in London and I had no way of contacting him.

We had moved to the outskirts of a small village in the countryside with hardly any neighbours and there was no one nearby that I could ask for help. We hadn't yet registered with a local doctor and I was frantically flicking through the *Yellow Pages*, trying to find one. Finally, I got through to an emergency doctor who said he'd be there in thirty minutes. Then, hesitatingly, I called my parents who were shocked at hearing my gasping voice.

At last, the doctor arrived and started treating me immediately, soon followed by my panic-stricken parents who fretted about, not knowing what to do. Eventually, an ambulance came and whisked me off to the nearest hospital. That was my very first experience of asthma and I'd just had the most horrendous attack.

By the time my dear parents were allowed into to see me at the hospital, I was already lying in bed, hooked up to a nebuliser and oxygen. I felt absolutely drained physically but was very relieved to be there. I'll never forget my father's agonised, helpless expression as he looked down at my mask-covered face, trying to make sense of it all. I had never let them know just how difficult and turbulent my life was since the wedding. How could I tell them the marriage was failing and that all we did was argue? After all, their marriage was not much different but they kept going. How could I possibly tell my mother, knowing how she would react? No doubt, she would be appalled and only scold me for stubbornly marrying someone I had chosen myself – a guy who was in no position to 'take care of me' – instead of letting them choose a 'well-educated, good Bengali boy'.

After five days in the hospital, I had had plenty of time to think and re-evaluate my life. However, I emerged not very much wiser, as I still needed to learn my lessons the hard way. The only thing I had decided was that instead of wrapping my life around Ted and all his needs, I would make a little more time to do some of the things I enjoyed and try to re-connect with my old friends.

Over the following months, the asthma kept flaring up and six months later, I had another big attack. Luckily, I didn't need to go into hospital as I had the necessary medication at home and by then, enough experience of how to deal with it. As I began to recover and had no one else to turn to, I found an old notebook and started to journal my turbulent thoughts. This was the beginning of my healing journey. Writing helped me to make sense of things and decide on my next steps, which I'll explain more about in Chapter Four.

It was only many years later that I was able to understand the significance of that illness which had taken over my throat and stopped me from breathing. It showed me just how dangerous it is to not address the ongoing hurt I had been swallowing down and that by repressing my emotions, it had led to physical illness. My body was raging at the torment of having my voice stifled and trying to tell me that the marriage was suffocating. This is a perfect example of how our outer worlds directly affect and reflect our inner worlds.

Another six months passed and finally, I made the most difficult and painful decision I had ever made; to leave the person I loved most and had promised to spend my life with. At the time, it seemed like the worst possible solution but there was no other way. Ted was a gentle, quiet, pleasant man with a creative soul and without a doubt, he did care about me but he was young and inexperienced. He didn't know how to be a supportive husband or partner and work together as a couple.

Despite the challenges, I still believed that a marriage was for life and this man was all I ever wanted. My fairy tale, which had gone somewhat sour, could still be mended and I was still determined to make it work. There was still hope that he might grow out of his bad habits and learn to be more considerate. I had allowed him to become very dependent on me and he had happily taken the passenger's seat in the relationship. "Maybe if I just let go a bit, it would give him the space to change, to let him mature", I decided.

I knew what I should do was release the reins. I had to let go of paying all the bills and rent, doing all the housework and putting food in our bellies. Most of our arguments were centred on him not making any financial contribution whilst I had two jobs, trying to make ends meet. I began to feel resentful as I realised that I had become a mother to him. It also dawned on me that I was of the least priority in his mind. "Perhaps when I am not around, he will be forced to take the reins and therefore, take more responsibility. He might even begin to value me more and appreciate all that I've been doing", I thought, clinging onto the last vestiges of hope.

Eventually, after much deliberation, I decided not to go 'cold turkey' but to be a little gentler on myself. Instead of leaving him completely, I would go away to work abroad for a while. I knew that moving somewhere across town – or even to the other side of the country – was not an option. The only way to keep myself from running back to him as soon as I felt lonely, sad or needy, would be to get out of the country. Of course, Ted hated the idea and didn't want me to leave. Eventually, after much pandering and persuasion, he conceded that a nine-month contract abroad was a relatively short time in the span of a lifetime together.

However, after going away and working for one stint abroad, I felt as though a decade had passed. When I returned, he was there at the airport, eagerly awaiting me with open arms. He hugged me warmly but strangely, I felt nothing in return. My body already knew what my heart and head refused to acknowledge.

Soon, I discovered he had not only squandered all the money I had sent home, but also used up my overdraft and got himself even further in to debt. The arguments started again and as usual, I always succumbed and forgave him. I went to the bank and opened another line of credit, in my name to help him out, which he promised to pay back within a few months. I was still hanging onto a glimmer of hope that the relationship might work, although deep down, my soul was calling me to run away again.

To Begin Again

When a relationship ends, it does not matter who lets whom go, for it is equally devastating. Leaving Ted was as painful for me, if not more so, than had he been the one to walk away from me. Taking that huge step was the most difficult decision I had ever made. But it was one of the best decisions I ever made.

Unfortunately, my romantic life did not improve much in the coming years and I would continue to get hurt, over and over again. Every time I would gather up the pieces of my broken heart, take them home and get out my magnifying glass to analyse it all. Each time I would try to understand what had gone wrong, conclude that I had done my best and try to learn the lesson.

During my youth and young adulthood, I hardly had any friends upon whom I could really lean on or completely trust to share my strange, convoluted world with. So I would never disclose anything about my private life to anyone. Instead, I did as many do; hide in my cave, alone, to cry and nurse my sorrows. Quite often, just a few months after a heartbreak, you would find me looking for sanctuary in the next relationship. But of course, as you know, that is never a good idea if you want to heal a broken heart.

So, what should I have done after the relationship had broken down? How do you keep going if your heart is lying in shreds and you just want to curl up and disappear? Where do you begin and how can you tackle the pain when your life has just fallen apart?

Most people turn to their friends, mothers, sisters or even colleagues to share the pain and relay everything about how their awful relationship came to an end. Some people will turn to anyone who might listen and tell them all the sordid details about their ex's activities, the terrible things he/she did, hurtful arguments, discrepancies, etc.

Certainly, the need to vent and unload is natural and human. It is perfectly normal that we should want to share our burdens when we have had tough times and need support. However, what many of us don't consider is that each time we share our story, in *vivid detail*, we paint a picture in our listeners' head. When you describe a nasty event or the horrid behaviour of your ex to someone else, that person then imagines the whole scenario, word-for-word in his/her head. This imaginary *recreating* then reinforces their beliefs about you, and of the kind of relationship and type of partner you tend to attract, and therefore, will probably *attract again*.

If that person is not a hundred percent on your side, his/her thoughts might be creating something even worse. Whilst listening with great interest to your story, he/she may well be quietly judging and blaming you but never showing it. As if that isn't bad enough, what neither of you may realise, is what she/he is subconsciously *feeling* towards you, and that this will affect and influence you too. The more time we spend focusing on and talking about all the sad, wrong and difficult experiences in our lives, especially when shared with negative people, the more likely it is that we will attract more of the same in the future.

To help you avoid speaking with such people, here is a more positive and beneficial method to start the process of healing your heart. Before taking any action or doing practical exercises, it is important to prepare yourself and have the right mindset, so I recommend that you take the time to consider the following Lesson before we dive into doing more in-depth self-work.

LESSON 1: Start Your Healing Journey

A. Set the Intention

Make an agreement with yourself that now, it is time to heal. Even if it has been a long time since you broke up from a relationship, decide that you will give yourself time to heal. If you had broken a bone, you would need time to rest and let it mend. Your heart needs the same, if not more, care, compassion and time to heal.

Don't rush the process with thoughts such as, 'get over it', 'he/she isn't worth my tears' or 'I must pull myself together and get on with normal life'. Instead, tell yourself the following:

- I now decide to give myself time to heal.
- I did the best I could with the knowledge, experience and support I had at that time.
- I did nothing wrong by falling in love.
- Just because things went wrong does not mean I made a mistake.
- I choose to create a better, healthier future.
- I am willing to do all that I need to do to heal my heart.

If you do not give yourself time to heal, the wounds in your heart will remain buried and only resurface the next time you are in a relationship. So, you will only end up attracting the same kind of relationship again and find yourself in the same predicament. Even if it takes many years for you to meet another person, the previous hurt and suffering will inevitably rise up and cause problems if it is not properly treated and released.

Perhaps, at this stage, you might think, 'never again' and shut the door to any future relationships altogether. However, if you don't allow your heart to heal, it may also affect other relationships such as those with your family, children, friends and colleagues. So decide now, that you do *deserve* to be whole, healthy and happy again no matter what the future holds.

B. Love is Blind

Remind yourself that falling in love is blind. Mother Nature designed us to 'lose our heads' when we first meet someone that we are really attracted to. Falling in love is supposed to be crazy, all-encompassing and completely overwhelming. It makes us feel anxious, irrational, exhilarated and entranced, all at the same time. We find ourselves in a state of 'enchantment' and we become someone unlike our usual sane or level-headed selves. To add to this mix of madness, we don't notice any faults about the object of our desire or question our hearts. In fact, we even find those silly little foibles about her/him, not in the least annoying, but utterly adorable.[2]

So, why do we behave in such ridiculous ways, unlike our normal selves? There is a good reason. Falling *in love* is not 'deep, true love'. At that early stage, it is rather like being 'in fascination' or under a magic spell. If we did not feel that all-encompassing madness at the outset of a relationship we might never actually create the bonds that make us love that person long term. However, as I am sure you know, the magic spell only lasts a spell and then, either grows into a much deeper, loving relationship or falters and dissipates. It is this crazy feeling that creates the momentum, desire and commitment that keeps a couple together. So, don't beat yourself up for having fallen for your ex. You did what is only natural and normal. Be kind to yourself, knowing that you only did exactly as Mother Nature intended for you to do.

C. Acceptance

Now, if you haven't done so yet, it is time to admit to yourself that the relationship is well and truly over and accept everything that happened. However, when you have invested so much of your time, effort, heart and soul into something, especially a relationship, the hardest thing to do is to let go of it from your heart. You may have physically walked away but it may take much, much longer to release it all mentally and emotionally.

There are many psychological and rational reasons why we hang onto a relationship in our heads and hearts. Often, if there are children, friends or other people we care about involved, it makes the process much more difficult.

It could be that you are still feeling very let down, betrayed and angry and so, want to give your ex a piece of your mind. Hence, the door is not yet closed and the relationship somehow, still feels 'unfinished'.

Sometimes, it could be that you are still unconsciously hoping for some kind of reconciliation. Despite our rational thinking and acceptance of the relationship being over, in our deepest hearts, we might still want to be back with that person.

If you are still finding it hard to accept that the relationship is over, try the following simple exercise every day, for at least a week. Stand in front of your mirror, look into your own eyes and say the following, out loud:

- I release and let (her/his name) go.
- I accept that the relationship is finished and over.
- Now, I am free and single.
- I fully accept my new status and situation.
- I know I am exactly where I need to be right now.

As you repeat these words aloud, you may feel a wave of emotion rise and flood your senses. That's okay. Just allow whatever you feel to come up. In the next chapter, we will discuss more about allowing yourself to feel all those difficult emotions and how to deal with them.

D. Talking and Sharing

When you feel overwhelmed by all that has happened, most probably, you will need to vent and talk about all that you've experienced. As I said, this is completely natural but before you do, take a few moments to consider the following questions about the person with whom you wish to share:

- Is this person 100% behind me and supportive of my decisions?
- How well has she/he supported me in the past?
- Can I trust her/him to keep what I say completely private?
- How does she/he usually make *me feel* when I disclose personal things?
- How will he/she think or react afterwards?
- How will what I say make him/her feel?

If your answers are positive and you are sure that you feel safe to confide in that person, then go ahead. Before you share your very private information, ensure that you can completely trust and rely upon that person to understand you and protect your best interests.

Be aware that unloading all your troubles can also result in upsetting your friend or relative, especially if she/he cares about you and that he/she will need your reassurance before you begin. You can prepare her/him by saying you need to talk and ask if she/he would kindly listen with a non-critical ear. Explain that you need to talk about painful and unpleasant things and you are not looking for answers or solutions.

At the end of the conversation, ensure you show gratitude and reassure him/her for supporting you. Request that she/he should not take onboard any negativity or feel responsible for your situation in any way.

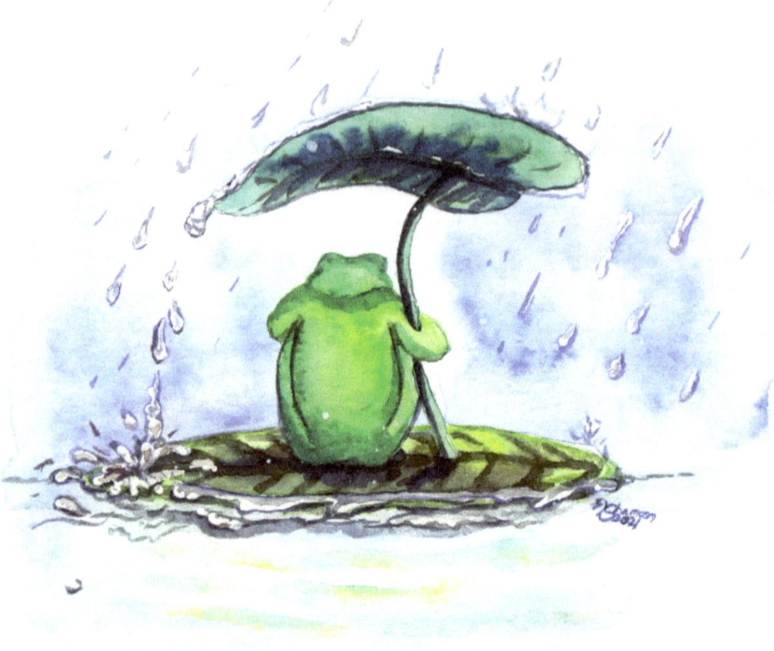

3. Rivers of Release

She had travelled far only to find herself utterly lost and forlorn. The path along the gloomy river wound endlessly into the distance.

"Oh, how much longer must I continue?" she thought, miserably. "I never once imagined that sailing away on an adventure would mean traipsing across such a wretched land."

Aching from head to foot, she rubbed her hungry belly and wished her fairy godmother would appear.

On and on through the foreboding forest she trudged, until at last she came across a great mango tree. "Oh, bountiful tree, may I please have a piece of your fruit?" she begged.
"Why, certainly," smiled the old tree and shook its branches letting some ripe mangoes fall to the ground. "Come, eat all you want and rest awhile under my branches as tomorrow, you must travel yet farther," said the tree. "But fear not, for soon, you shall find your true path."

The Toad Prince

Despite being surrounded by people throughout my young life, there were few that knew anything of my private world. From an early age, I had learned that no one cared much about my tears and so any crying was done alone, shut in the bathroom. I had grown up knowing I would only be ridiculed for showing my tears and that it was a sign of weakness.

By the time I had reached adulthood, hiding my pain had become a well-honed skill and the outside world only ever saw my jovial mask of fun and frivolity. In truth, I had no idea how to lean on others and hence, learned to be very independent, always pulling myself up by my 'own bootstraps' out of any difficult or painful situation. I never knew how or with whom to seek support. Moreover, I never allowed myself to feel sadness for very long. It was only many, many years later that I was able to fully appreciate the purpose and healing strength of crying and grieving.

My life had come to a stop the year my dear father passed away. I was already struggling to find a job and trying to get my life back together after my previous relationship had fallen apart. It had all mounted up leaving my heart, mind and soul shattered. At the age of forty, my inner world had begun to crumble as I fell deeper into a depression. Finally, I admitted that I needed support and went to the doctor. But neither medication nor a course of counselling sessions could help me find the answers I needed. There was a deep gnawing pain which refused to shift and a growing sadness that continued to weigh me down.

A couple of years passed as I inched my way back to some normality and managed to find a good job back in my home town. Life was passing by quickly and soon I found myself looking online again. Despite the many failed Internet 'matches', I was still allowing myself to be distracted by looking at dating sites. I found one 'for professionals' and started chatting to one or two appropriate contenders. At the time, I wasn't whole-heartedly looking, so when I met Rick, I was over the moon! From the moment I laid eyes on him, I felt that at last, this was definitely Mr Right, my prince had arrived!

As I stared at the photo that smiled back at me from my computer screen, there was a strange feeling of recognition, of already knowing this man. His profile matched my wishes perfectly. He seemed to have the right background, the same values and beliefs, and he wanted the same things from a relationship. After a few weeks of communicating online and some phone calls, we started dating.

Everything seemed to be fine at first, but as time went on, we seemed to disagree more and more. It was as though I couldn't do anything right, and he would get awfully angry about some little thing I had done or said. I discovered that Rick had a short temper, and without warning, he would flare up and blame me for insignificant things. It felt as though I was always walking on eggshells and had to tiptoe around him.

One evening, after returning from an enjoyable day out at a friend's wedding, he suddenly flipped from 'Jekyll to Hyde' over something I'd said that was quite trivial. In an instant, he became furious and verbally aggressive towards me. After an explosive argument and without warning, he suddenly decided that he'd had enough – it was over! He didn't want to see me anymore!

I was aghast and caught off guard. "What, really?! No! You're not serious?!" I spluttered, stunned and confused. Was it something we ate at the wedding? Had my prince taken a bite from some poison apple and turned into a raging ugly toad? I felt as though I had been dropped from the sky onto cold, hard concrete. I was choked and shocked by his enraged reaction. "B-b-but w-w-why? How c-c-can you say that?" I stuttered, pleading pathetically and asking him to change his mind, but he was adamant that I had ruined everything and it was all my fault.

I stumbled out of his apartment in tears of despair and disbelief, and drove home, absolutely devastated. "How could he just dump me like that – for no good reason?! No, no, no! This can't be happening..." My heart lay in tatters; my mind was a blur of questions and confusion. "Surely, he will recover from this delirium? Yes, of course, he will change his mind eventually, when he comes to his senses." I tried to calm myself but felt more lost than ever and could not comprehend how he could be so cruel.

For four long months, I cried and agonised, my emotions in turmoil and longed to be with him again. "I really thought that we were meant to be. Isn't he supposed to be the *one*? The one I had always dreamed of?" I thought trying to make sense of it all but still could not fathom why he had let me go. I tried to meditate and look deep into my soul for the answers. All I knew was that I had to keep going and trust that there was a good reason for his madness. My intuition kept saying that I must have faith and things would eventually get better. "Maybe one day, when he is ready, he will come back to me," I consoled myself, clinging to a small glimmer of hope; the only thing that kept my heart beating.

Months passed by, then, one day, I decided it was time to visit Rick again. "He must have realised by now, after all this time, that he is still in love with me and we are meant to be," I decided, trying to boost my deflated confidence. I prepared carefully, rehearsed what to say and lovingly wrapped the special, handmade gift I'd spent hours making. "Surely, he will come to his senses again, when he sees me! Surely, he will remember how great we are together and be delighted to be with me. Well, at least, I must try. It's now or never."

As I stood outside the entrance to his apartment block, my heart pounded in my ears. I took a deep breath and hesitantly pressed the buzzer to his apartment, waiting for his voice. He was surprised and annoyed to hear me. Why had I just shown up unannounced?
"Can we just talk, please? Just for a few minutes? I've come such a long way..." I begged till he agreed.

I climbed the three flights of stairs, praying things would work out but when I arrived at his door, his irritation was obvious. Grudgingly, he let me in, made some tea and sat tentatively on the arm of a sofa, foot twitching and frowning down at me.

Twenty minutes later, I sat in my car, my head on the steering wheel, crying like a child, hot tears streaming down my face. When I had tried to explain how I felt about him, his volcano erupted again but this time much worse than when we had last parted. After I mentioned the word 'love' to him, his fuse blew. "How dare you come here uninvited, trespassing upon my life!" he shouted, "How dare you say you love me?! Who do you think you are?! Get out, GET OUT!"

Nothing I could say would make him calm down, change his mind or see sense. In all my years of being in relationships, I had never experienced such anger and hostility. I was afraid he might get physically violent and attack me. I fled, staggering down the stairs as my knees wobbled, feeling utterly bewildered and still clutching the gift which he had refused to take.

Shaking and sobbing with humiliation, I sat in my car in a daze. I was too shocked to drive and allowed the emotions to rise up and take over. I must have cried for a solid ten or fifteen minutes. It all seemed too surreal to be happening. I pleaded with the gods, "Tell me, please, what is going on? What have I done that is so wrong?" A few moments later, the storm thundering inside me suddenly stopped and a strange feeling washed over me. As though a ray of sunshine had beamed through the dark clouds, it melted away my torment and dried up the tears. Like a wave from a magic wand, it began to dawn on me that the relationship was now, definitely over, finally.

I took several deep, life-affirming breaths and blew them out of the open window, releasing a lungful of heartache with each one. I waited for another bait of tears to overwhelm me but interestingly, nothing happened. I sat, expecting those habitual feelings to return, the longing and needing to be with Rick, but none came back. They were all gone! As I breathed, it felt as though a physical weight had been lifted off my chest.

The yearning to be back with him, that heavy feeling I had carried for so long, was simply gone. He had destroyed it all, quite literally, by slamming the door and throwing me out. I finally accepted that the door of any possibility of 'us' ever being together again was now, firmly closed. "Now, I guess it really is over", I said aloud. "There's no going back…ever." As if a curse was suddenly lifted, I began to feel lighter and freer. I gathered myself together and went to the nearest cafe, got a nice hot coffee-to-go and drove the two-hour journey home, calmly and dry-eyed.

River of Tears

As this relationship came to an end, it was as though a deep, forgotten well had been unearthed inside me. Rick was definitely not Mr Right but he was the right catalyst I needed to begin the process of grieving. Over the coming months, I cried again and again… a lot. I found myself sitting on the sofa and crying alone for hours and hours. I shut down from social life, went into 'my cave' and only came out to go to work or buy food. This involuntary deluge of tears was quite unexpected and certainly not something that I had ever experienced before.

Instead of stifling it as I had always done in the past, I decided to allow it. I said to myself, "If that's how you feel, then let yourself *feel*. Go ahead and cry. Let it out. After all, isn't that what you would suggest to a client in the same situation?" And so, I cried and cried. "Hell – I don't care anymore! I am tired of trying to be strong. Tired of always trying to be calm and in control. I'm just going to let myself feel everything! Whatever my system wants to do, I'm just going to let it do," I decided.

For what seemed like decades, the crying continued. Sometimes they were full-on blasts of uncontrollable sobbing and at other times, quiet, slow tears rolled down my unmoving face as I did the dishes. In between, there were periods of complete unemotional numbness that left me utterly bereft and without any feeling.

Today, I wonder how I managed to get through that dreadfully sad year of my life because I still got up every day, went to work and did a good job. I pulled on my 'smiley' mask as I drove to work and throughout the day, no one was any the wiser. Then, as soon as I left the office and found myself alone again, the tears would start. It was as though a great dam, which had been blocked for centuries, finally burst open and was flooding a dried out river.

You may be thinking, "Why all that crying?" It was certainly not for the loss of Rick and that toxic relationship. At first, I wasn't sure what was happening to me but as time passed, I became aware that it was the years and years of unspent grieving that I had buried away which was now coming to the surface.

The princess had, unwittingly, drunk the potion that now sent her sinking into her own stream of tears and was now being washed down a winding river to God-only-knows where. She found herself grieving for the little girl who had bottled up all of her tears because she thought she ought to be **strong**. *She shed buckets of tears for that lonely, unsupported teenager and her unrequited love. She wept for the young woman who had married for all the wrong reasons and just wanted to please her parents. She mourned for all the unhappy relationships she had pursued for years and years, because she had undervalued herself. She sobbed sorrowfully for the disappointment after disappointment her poor heart had endured whilst having to manage all that pain alone.*

Alas, she knew not where the river would lead but trusted that there was still magic in this world and that there must be a purpose for her torment. And thus, she gained a little strength with which to carry on.

There were times when I stood in my garden with a cigarette, staring up at the dismal sky, shaking a fist at the gods, quietly shouting, "Why, after all these years, did I have to go through this hell now?! Why had I failed time and time again? Isn't it enough failure for one person to contend with?" My emotions led me wading through seas of anger, frustration, pain, hopelessness and absolute misery.

For me, this overwhelming sadness that had risen up from the depths and flooded my senses was hard to explain or share with anyone. I did have a few trusted, dependable friends whom I knew I could turn to, if need be, but I felt I must walk this path alone. It seemed as though I was crawling through a deep, dark tunnel with no light at the other end. I had no idea how long it would take, whether I would ever come out of it or if there would be any future at all ahead of me.

Each night, when the crying was done, I would fall asleep exhausted. And in those moments, just before sleep, I sometimes felt a tiny flicker of positivity; like a whisper that came up from the darkness, telling me, "You'll be okay. Keep going. There is a good reason for all this. Just *trust*."

The Grieving Process

The first hurdle for me was to accept that it was okay to cry. Until that point in my life, I had never given myself full permission to let go, be vulnerable and allow myself to feel all those unhappy emotions. If you think you have been doing the same, be warned; when left unchecked, that dragon will come back to bite you. Please, do not push down your negative emotions for years and years as I did because, inevitably, they will resurface sooner or later, with a vengeance.

I decided that, despite my normal positive, happy disposition, if these unwelcome, depressing feelings were insisting on coming up, then I should let them. This wave of grieving each day was certainly not something I was forcing, making up or would choose to spend my time doing. But it was *very* real. Nature has a reason for everything so at the time, it felt right to not deny this natural urge.

My logical thinking and psychological understanding pointed to the fact that if such strong emotions were arising, they must need to be expressed and released. It is equally human to feel sadness and anger as it is to feel gladness and joy. Therefore, why should we allow one and not the other?

When a relationship breaks down, it is akin to experiencing the death of a loved one. Sometimes, it can be even more painful because death is usually not a choice we make but breaking up a relationship is. Social conditioning teaches us to believe that all those difficult, painful emotions are bad and should be subdued. On the contrary, they should be expressed and released out of our system in an appropriate way. Otherwise, they can end up causing, not only depression, but also anxiety, fear, physical sickness and long term ill health.[3]

Grieving is a process, and according to psychological theory, there are five stages to the experience of loss (see figure 1). The length of time it takes to go through each stage varies greatly from one person to another. The way we experience grief, depends on our learnt coping strategies, individual personalities and specific circumstances.

Figure 1: Kübler-Ross Grief Cycle

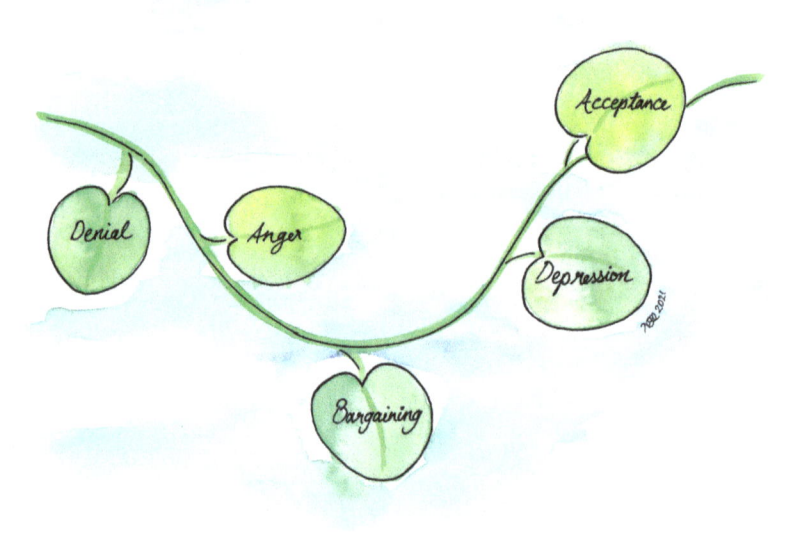

Also, it may not always be a linear process and we may jump back and forth between the stages. At the beginning, you may experience any number of different emotions, such as anger, hate, vengefulness, guilt, shame, numbness or desperation. You may continue to feel different degrees of these emotions arising long after the grieving process is over.

A word of warning: if you find yourself feeling resentful and wanting to avenge your ex-partner, bear in mind that the effects of carrying out an act of vengeance will be far more detrimental to yourself rather than your ex. When you dwell on causing harm or doing something negative to another person, your subconscious mind will automatically attract more harmful or negative states to you rather than the other person, which can manifest in your internal or external world in many ways. I will explain more about manifestation in the coming chapters. For the sake of your own health and wellbeing, it is much better to find methods to release these emotions without seeking or wishing harm upon your ex or anyone else. In Chapter Eight, I will give you some very effective ways to do this.

As I learnt to trust the process and express all the buried emotions, I began to let go of all the related negative baggage which I had carried for so many years. In previous relationships, I remember always feeling there was something lacking. This was an indication of my own underlying pain, sadness and deep-down, fear. My lack of self-worth and the mountain of suppressed grief had attracted partners that reflected similar *lack* in their lives.

Whilst going through that dark tunnel, I had completely lost sight of my normal, natural happy self over those long, miserable months. It was only thanks to my complete faith that things would work out for the better, and my knowledge about the grieving process, that kept me sane. Within a year of coming out of that tunnel, my life had changed dramatically for the better. Although it was an incredibly tough journey, it was an absolutely necessary one. I have since realised that if I hadn't allowed myself that time to grieve, I would have spiralled into a deeper depression and possible illness. Not only did it help my mental and emotional health, but it also cleared the path for my future joy-filled life.

LESSON 2: Purge the Pain

A. Purpose of Grieving

You might think that you have no need to grieve because you dealt with all of that stuff a long time ago. It's been many years since your relationship ended and it is all past history. If so, that is good news and you can skip this part. However, this exercise is for you if you are unsure and have questions, such as:

- How do I know if I need to grieve?
- What if I don't know whether I am actually *over* that person?

In this case, try asking yourself the following questions. Write down the answers in your notebook as spontaneously as possible, without thinking too much.

1. Do I often cry or get emotional over small things?
2. Do I easily get upset watching an emotional scene on TV?
3. Does it feel as though my bubble of positivity will burst if someone just pokes it?
4. Do I feel like I am often masking or covering up my true feelings?
5. Do I often get overly angry or 'worked up' over day-to-day situations?
6. Do I dislike being quiet and tend to talk a lot. Or do I always switch on the TV or music to fill the space?
7. Do I hate noise and feel unsettled when too many people are talking around me?
8. Does thinking about my ex make me get emotional? (Good or bad feelings)

9. If I think about a possible future relationship, am I reminded of all past hurts or troubles?
10. Have I shut out the possibility of a future relationship for many years?
11. Have I jumped into relationships too soon following a break-up?

If your answers are mainly yes, then you are most likely repressing some emotions and holding onto unspent grief.

B. Grieving Session

In most modern societies, we are taught very little about grief or grieving and given few tools of how to cope with it. This is a simple method to help you release any grief you might have pushed down and perhaps, did not know how to express.

1. First, prepare a safe, physical space. It is probably best done in your own home. Make a time for yourself and switch off your TV, phone and all external disturbances. Depending on your individual preference, you can choose whether you want a supportive person present or to do this alone.
2. Sit down, take a few deep breaths and close your eyes. Take your mind back to your ex and the previous relationship. Spend a few minutes allowing yourself to remember any particular situation that comes to mind and the things that happened at that time.
3. Open your eyes. If you feel angry, be angry. If you feel sad, be sad. If you feel like crying, let yourself cry. Give yourself permission to feel whatever emotions that may arise. If you want to punch a pillow, stamp your feet, pace about, scream or shout, do so. As long as you do not cause harm to yourself or anyone else, go ahead and allow yourself to express all that you are feeling. Take as much time as you need.

4. Tell yourself it is okay to feel these feelings and let them out. Acknowledge that these are *your* feelings and you want to be rid of them. Accept that these are just emotions which will pass.
5. Do not force, do not push, do not try to 'work at it'. This is simply an experience that should come up naturally from within.
6. Be aware that you are stepping out of your 'comfort zone' and your own feelings may seem confusing, alarming or peculiar at first. Remind yourself by saying these words, "I trust myself. I trust this process. I know that this releasing is healing me."

Your grieving session may take ten minutes or several hours but you will know when you have had enough. Depending on how much you need to release, you should repeat this exercise as often as you feel capable of handling it. Eventually, you will get to a stage when you no longer have such strong feelings coming up. You will be able to think and talk about your ex without having all those negative emotions and just feel neutral about her/him.

After a while, the heaviness of expressing and releasing all that sadness, anger and frustration will start to dissipate. You will notice that you begin to feel lighter and freer as you go through the stages of grief. This will indicate that you are coming to the end of this unpleasant but essential journey.

Now, you are probably asking, "Does it really have to be so tough? Can't I just do a little bit and be done with it?" Grieving is never easy, and if you don't go through the process, it will fester like a sore wound deep inside you. However, be reassured that it is quite safe and nothing sinister will happen to you when you choose to express all those negative emotions. You will get through this and come out at the other end, so don't be afraid. The important point to remember is to just allow yourself to experience it and not stifle your feelings anymore.

However, if you do not take the time to go through this crucial process, the unexpressed grief will weigh you down mentally and emotionally, no matter how well you are able to mask it. It can jeopardise, hurt and taint any new relationship you might have in the future. I have seen anger, hate and sadness stemming from a broken heart, become twisted into a lifelong bitterness and later unleash itself upon partners, children and loved ones. I have also seen suppressed resentment, guilt and depression turn into years of struggle in a marriage and illnesses such as a debilitating cancer.

Therefore, it is better to take some time now to allow yourself to grieve, let it all go and heal rather than struggle with it for a lifetime. In the next chapter, you will find more ways to make the grieving process easier and new tools, which will uplift your inner self and lighten the load of this part of your journey.

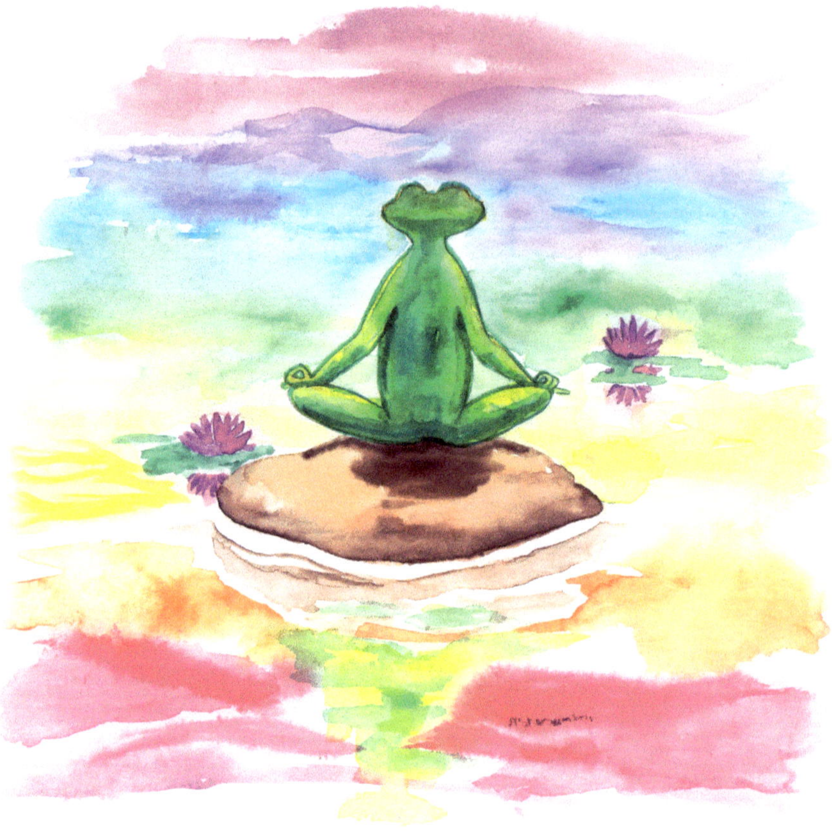

4. Sitting on a Rock

Alas, after many voyages to faraway lands, there was still no treasure to be found. Her ship had docked at yet another island which had nothing to offer but a big old conch shell. She sat down upon the sand to ponder and gaze out at the great ocean. Soon, she drifted off into a beautiful reverie of sun-kissed dreams.

As dusk approached, she opened her eyes and realised she must hurry back before the ship sails. "Oh dear, where did the hours go?" she yawned. "I haven't done any digging today".

Looking down at the conch shell lying in the sand beside her, she said, "Well, I suppose this'll have to do. You shall be my treasure."
"Why, yes, indeed. I am the treasure you've always desired, my lady." replied a tiny voice.
The princess was startled. "Oh my! Did you just speak?" she asked, holding up the shell to her ear.
"Yes, t'was I," said the tiny voice. "I've been here all along, waiting patiently for you. You had only to look inside."

Bon Voyage

When I started looking for a job that could take me abroad, I applied for everything I could find, from holiday reps and tour guides to au pairs and flight attendants. By then, I had acquired plenty of work experience and felt confident about the skills I could offer an employer. I did not doubt my ability in getting a job as I had always been quite successful at interviews. It was just a question of finding the right job for me. My self-assuredness about interviews also came from practising a special *mind exercise* that always helped me and which I will share with you in the coming chapters. Unfortunately, that unwavering confidence in my work life did not spill over into my love life. Well, not yet.

So, as you can imagine, landing a job to work on cruise ships was a dream come true. Being a travel lover, it was an opportunity I simply could not pass up. It made the perfect excuse for me to persuade Ted that I wanted to go abroad for a while. After I received the job offer, there was little time to think and I busied myself with making all the arrangements for my journey. I would be away for one contract, usually nine months long, and I was incredibly excited.

It was June 1994, and with a heavy but hopeful heart, I stepped out of Miami Airport and was greeted by a blast of warm, tropical air. After a typical downpour in the summer, it was always hot and sticky but I soon got used to it. Alone in an unfamiliar new country, I had little time to spend worrying about Ted and all that I had left behind. The next day, I had to find my way to the company's head office and get relevant documents, uniforms and medical checks all sorted out. Then, the first few days aboard my ship were spent settling in, getting to know my way around, and learning 'the ropes' and extensive safety regulations.

Within a few weeks, the princess had merged easily and anonymously into the mass of crew, slipping easily into a routine of long work hours and socialising onboard. The happy, smiling photos of herself with her friends at beautiful Caribbean ports, which she pinned above her bunk, belied the truth of her secret sadness. On the surface, no one would ever have guessed anything was wrong for they would only see her vivacious, joyful façade. But almost every night, aching with the emptiness in her heart, she would cry herself to sleep in silence.

At work, I put on my brave, professional mask, and as nobody knew anything about me or my past, it was easy to hide it all. Working in the gift shop meant providing 'service with a smile', no matter what might be going on in our personal lives. I let myself be absorbed in doing my job, keeping busy and thinking only about the present moment. After work, the onboard social life took over, crowding out any thoughts about home and all sad emotions were pushed down below decks.

Finally, I could do as I wanted without getting stressed about the rent, bills, cooking and cleaning... or thinking about how much I missed Ted. I could drink, smoke, dance, party, have fun and stay out as late as I wanted without any restrictions. Being on ships reminded me of a scene from an old comedy, a Laurel and Hardy film in which they joined the French Foreign Legion because they wanted to forget![4]

However, I didn't forget. I simply hid the pain and torment that lay deep in my heart. It was carefully concealed with large portions of laughter, being with friends, seeing sites and working hard. Taking myself away to a foreign environment and diving into a hectic lifestyle meant that I did not give myself the chance to think, heal or grieve fully. At that time, I did not understand just how bad the effects of suppressing my feelings would be or their long term consequences. Pretending all was well in my life had become second nature. I faked it so well that I wasn't even aware of just how hurt I was inside or what I actually felt deep down, underneath it all. Interestingly, however, during the whole time on the ships, I did not once suffer from asthma again, despite taking up smoking cigarettes.

Making Me Time

My family and culture had taught me that long hours of toil were needed if one was to achieve happiness or success in life. There was little time for play in childhood and having fun was considered unproductive as my father disapproved of lethargy. Therefore, as long as I was occupied, it meant that I must be doing well. I learned to expertly play the role of always looking busy; acting as though I was always doing something valuable and necessary. I played 'being productive' so well, to the point that I actually believed it myself. Of course, this was a *default program* which ran for many years throughout my adult life, which I didn't recognise it until I had reached my forties. By 'default program', I refer to those automatic thoughts and habitual behaviours we all naturally have and do without consciously being aware.

However, one essential and healthy habit I acquired whilst on the ships was to give myself 'time out', something which I had never done before. It was vital for the healing I needed and growing my level of self-worth. If I hadn't taken the time to relax, the constant socialising and being in a people-centred job would have driven me crazy. I grew to accept, appreciate and relish the short excursions I took alone. Soon, it became a necessity to get away from all the passengers and crew whenever I had a little spare time, in order to recharge and be with myself.

During every cruise, we would dock at various ports and, as crew members, we were privy to the many non-touristy areas with hidden coves, quiet walks and 'locals only' cafes. So, I would take myself off to some unfrequented spot and enjoy a few hours of solitude and contemplation.

For the first time in my life, I was able to reflect upon and recognise my own needs and wants in life. I would sit in quiet cafes or at the beach and write in my journal. As I felt I had no one to rely on that I could share my private thoughts with, my journal became my only confidant, comfort and place to vent. I wrote to pour my heart out and 'unload' all the worries, sadness, frustrations and longings onto paper. Afterwards, I would always feel a greater sense of relief, which I knew I could never get from trying to talk about it with someone.

My favourite place was sitting under a palm tree somewhere quiet, away from everyone else. There, I would close my eyes behind my sunglasses and listen to the waves as I meditated. It was the only way I was able to hear my own thoughts, let go of the heaviness and breathe in the calming, soothing, regenerating energy of Mother Nature. Eventually, I began to understand the truth and receive answers to all of the questions that had plagued me for years. I call this process 'sitting on my rock' and it is still one of my favourite ways to nurture myself. It is only when we are still and alone that we can hear the whispers of wisdom that come up from deep within us; our all-knowing soul-self.

When we came into our home port each week, I would go to the 'Call Station' to phone Ted, reassure him and catch up with all that was going on. After several months, the sadness began to fade and I started to feel more in balance and at peace inside myself.

Then, something quite unexpected happened: a long-forgotten feeling began stirring inside me, which I had not felt for a long, long time. I found myself noticing and being attracted to other men. "No, no, no!

This was not the idea!" I thought, aghast and appalled at myself. It was a terrible realisation and certainly, not one for which I'd planned. It sent me into a spate of self-contempt, anguish and confusion. According to my naïve, idealistic standards, this kind of thing was immoral and dishonest. I scolded myself and pushed away those thoughts for as long as I could.

Facing Facts

The biggest question, which I had been avoiding and pushed down to the basement, still lay heavily in my heart. It was now the summer of 1995, and I had taken a second contract to work on cruise ships. Over a year had passed since leaving home and the buried truth of what was actually happening inside me finally came to light. One late night, after most of the crew were asleep, I sat in my cabin, chatting with my roommate, Cherie. She had recently become a good friend, one of the very few I could really trust. The next day was probably a port day as we weren't worried about getting up early for work. So, we sat on the floor in our pyjamas, sharing a leisurely hot drink, little snacks and a good heart to heart.

Cherie was a great listener and for the first time, I found myself revealing my past and my reasons for leaving home to work on the ships. Her eyes widened in disbelief as I recounted my history and the life that I had left behind. I told her about how I dated Ted behind my parents' backs, the religious reasons for the Akht ceremony and that I still wasn't fully married according to civil law but still was a 'Miss' and not 'Mrs'. She listened intently as I told her about the social and cultural pressures, the turbulent relationship and how I made the toughest decision ever. She asked if I would ever go back to him. "Well, I am still married, so yes, probably... I think so", I replied.

After I had finished pouring out my long, sad saga, Cherie pondered for a while and eventually said, "Well, I have just one question: do you *love* him?" It was a simple, straightforward question and the answer should have been equally simple and straightforward.

I stared back at her blankly for a while, searching for the right words. "Good question," I replied hesitantly. "Hmm... well, yeah... I suppose I do," I said with an unconvincing expression.

I spent several days agonising over my answer. "Am I in love with him or in love with the *idea* of being in a marriage with him? Of course, I still loved him... but is it real love? If it isn't real love, what kind of love is it? Or am I simply holding on because of the promises I made and all the time we've invested together?" I tormented myself with more questions. "What about our families? After all, Ted had gone through all that hassle and accepted Islam as his own faith, just for me. Don't I owe him something for that? And I can't possibly leave him and disgrace my family! What if they disown me?" I interrogated myself, laying awake for hours and writing down everything in my journal, trying to analyse my feelings to get to the truth. My answers would be crucial because they would inevitably, determine the course of my life.

Eventually, after meditating, digging deep into my psyche, and much anxious worrying, it suddenly dawned on me that the very act of so much ruminating and self-questioning had actually given way to the truth. If I honestly still felt *true love* for him, I should have answered Cherie with a spontaneous and resounding, 'Yes!' There would have been nothing to question. I would not have been deliberating for days and days, trying to figure it out. I realised that my actual feelings for him were something more akin to still 'deeply caring' rather than loving him. The real reason I was hanging on to the relationship, was out of a strong sense of duty and obligation. These came from a need to keep my promises to him, to our parents and adhere to the cultural beliefs I had grown up with.

As my awareness grew and the truth became clear about my deeper feelings, the anguish returned to the surface and once again, I was engulfed in the pain and turmoil of knowing I had to let him go. Some more days passed and finally, with profound sadness, I faced my reality, accepting the inevitable next step. It was time to cut the chains for good. I waited till the ship had arrived at the next port, went to the telephone station and made those all-important calls, firstly, to my mother and then Ted. I gritted my teeth and steeled myself, ready for the volcanic eruptions.

Incredibly, my mother's reaction was not at all as I expected. She listened calmly to my explanations about my thoughts, worries, realisations and eventual decision.

"What do you think?" I asked nervously.

She was quiet for a few moments, then simply said, "Just go ahead, do what you must do and don't worry. I will take care of things at this end and talk to him when I see him next". I was totally surprised by her calmness and understanding. I was not used to confiding in my mother and was very grateful for her uncomplicated reassurance. At that moment, her acceptance was all that I needed to move on.

Unsurprisingly, Ted was horrified and became quite angry at me. He was infuriated that I would not come back to him and argued vehemently. He blamed me for all that had gone wrong in our relationship. I should never have gone away in the first place! When I told him I would no longer send money back home, he was absolutely furious. I let him rant for a while, knowing I'd hurt his pride, but held my ground and did not back down. There was no point arguing back; he would never accept my reasons.

Several months later, after I returned home, I went to his place to gather my belongings. He was still in disbelief, thinking that I would change my mind and expecting me to come running back. But my whole being, mind, body and soul, simply said 'No'. One thing was very clear: he was never going to change from being obstinate and self-centred. More importantly, I had grown and changed in ways that no longer wanted what little he had to offer. I had started to value my needs and learned some crucial lessons in life. Never again, would I go back to being a doormat and taken for granted by anyone, ever.

Going Inside

After her many journeys, the princess returned from her travels, weary but glad to be on dry land again. The princess had yet to learn that the few treasures she had acquired were indeed valuable. Now, all of her old friends and acquaintances had disappeared, and the few new friends she had made were left far behind in distant lands. Life at her family home had since, changed dramatically and her parents and siblings were all gone. They had moved away to study or travel and were all far too busy with their own lives to be concerned about hers. She found herself single again and with no one around that she 'needed to please', life could begin anew. The old chapter was definitively over. It was time to follow her heart and pursue her true destiny.

With the money I had manage to save, I happily bought myself a little second-hand car, updated my CV and took the best job I could find. Very soon, I moved into a one-bedroom apartment in a nearby village, close to my family home. The freedom was wonderful! It was utterly liberating and something I had never known before; a place to call my own. Growing up around a big family meant sharing a bedroom with my sister, and until then, I always had to share my belongings and space with others.

Returning from the very crowded ship environment where I shared a tiny cabin with no windows to having a whole apartment all to myself was an absolute luxury. My things remained exactly where I had left them in the morning and no one would steal my soap or use my towel. I could keep the place clean and tidy and at last, I had space to breathe.

Nights spent watching TV and eating dinner alone was a little strange at first but I relished not having to think about any other person. Apart from going to work, I could go for walks in nature, explore the local town and browse the little stores nearby. Being in solitude was complete bliss.

At last, there was quiet and plenty of time to contemplate all that had happened in my life. As well as gaining clarity and hearing the whispers of truth come through from my journal notes, I used another method to help me make sense of it all: I began to develop the art of 'going inside' myself and listening to my thoughts.

Part of my daily routine had always included prayer and meditation. When I say 'prayer', I don't mean anything religious, ritualistic or getting down on my knees. Neither do I mean sitting for long hours in Zen-like stillness when I talk about meditation. It was more of what I like to call, 'having a chat with God', and it is something I'd been doing since childhood. God was like a good friend and I would sit up in bed, get cosy with my hot water bottle, have a chat about the day and give thanks. It was as though I was talking to a real person sitting on the bed with me.

This relationship or connection with the Universal energy has always been, I believe, the main source of my strength, resilience and stability throughout my life. These chats have never been about begging the Almighty for help with anything *I* wanted. Perhaps, I would only ask for things such as peace and prosperity for my loved ones or help for those who might need it. Instead, whenever I wanted something for myself, I used a special method of, what was once called, 'dynamic meditation', that combines deep relaxation along with 'auto-suggestion' and visualisation.

I learned how to use this technique on a course, called the 'Silva Mind Method' when I was just eighteen.[5] My father first came across it in London and was so enthralled with it, he went on to become an instructor and later, gained a great following as the country director of Bangladesh. In my family, I was the only one who fully embraced the method and over the years, I have adapted and mastered it to suit my needs. Today, I am proud to say that it has, not only helped me navigate every challenge but also, laid the foundations for my teachings and helped me create a wonderful, fulfilling life.

Using this visualisation method, I have manifested countless things that have appeared in my life, such as finding the right car, home or job, as well as getting answers to difficult questions and dilemmas. For instance, I have posed questions such as how I should handle a difficult person or whether to accept a date or take an offer. Invariably, the right answer will come, either immediately or a day or two later. Then, it's up to me as to whether I act upon it.

This type of meditative visualisation has nothing to do with religion, and you don't need to follow any particular faith. I have found it to be far more powerful than just prayer or asking God for something. It harnesses the innate power of your mind by accessing the subconscious brain. When you practise this type of meditation, you can connect to your body, heart and soul. It is the starting platform for creating and attracting what you want in life. It helps you tune into your intuition and hear that all-important inner voice. Your inner self usually knows exactly what is good for you, which direction to take and even how to get there.

If you are spiritual or follow a faith, you may like to think of this inner voice as a saint, prophet, your guardian angel or a spirit guide that communicates with you and thus, you can easily integrate this method into your belief system. However, it is not necessary to have a religious faith, and it does not matter what label you chose to give it, as the method can help anyone calm their mind, relieve tension and release worries. This practice will benefit you in numerous ways, whether you are new to meditation or have had plenty of experience.

Meditating regularly, can not only calm your mind but also, lower stress levels, help mend relationships, and even find answers regarding anything that might be on your mind. Now, I will show you how to start developing this amazing inner ability and start practising using your natural inner wisdom, to heal the sadness of a broken heart and pave the way to much happier life. Once you get used to hearing your inner thoughts in this way, you can begin to use them for many purposes as well as manifesting your dreams for the future, and I will show you just how in the coming chapters.

LESSON 3: Create Calm

A. Heart Healing Meditation

This is a simple form of meditation that will allow you to tune into your natural healing system and which you can practise regularly. I recommend you choose a time either at night before bed, early in the morning after waking up, or possibly in the afternoon, after lunch, when you are naturally relaxed.

Find a place where you will not be disturbed. You may like to listen to some relaxing music whilst doing this exercise and you can find innumerable recordings available on the Internet.[6]

1. Sit or lie down in a comfortable position, ensuring your head and back are well supported.
2. Take three long, deep breaths and with each breath, feel yourself becoming more relaxed.
3. Count backwards slowly from 10 to 1, and with each number, focus on a part of your body and let it relax. Start with your feet and slowly work your way up to your head.
4. Feel your whole body relax. Relax your shoulders, face, eyes and jaw muscles. Tell yourself you are now deeply relaxed.
5. Imagine you are alone and taking a walk along the beach or beside a river or lake. It is a calm, beautiful day and the weather is perfect. You are at peace.
6. Look around and take in the scene with all your senses. You now stop at the water's edge and enjoy all that you see, feel, hear and smell.
7. Bring to mind your previous relationship and any negative emotions you may still be carrying. Imagine the sadness, pain or resentment as a physical thing somewhere inside your body. You may see a colour,

shape or feel a sense of heaviness. Now, imagine taking this negative emotion out of your body and throwing it into the water. Pull it out from inside you like a blob or cloud of darkness and as it falls into the water, see it dissolving, melting and being neutralised by the waves. The cloud or blob has now completely vanished.

8. Now, imagine taking off your shoes and stepping into the water yourself. The temperature feels just perfect and soothes your feet.

9. It is time to wash away what is left of that past relationship. You can either dive into the water, have a warm raincloud shower you or just crouch down and let the waves gently wash over you. This water is now cleansing away any remaining hurt, sadness or longing you might have. It is washing away all remnants of that relationship.

10. Imagine all those negative emotions are now gone. Tell yourself, "I am so glad to be rid of all that unnecessary stuff. I am healed, revived and free again," and step out of the water.

11. Feel the warm sunshine drying your skin. Imagine the sunlight as a healing energy on your skin and let it sink into your body. The sunlight flows through you, healing your mind, body and spirit. This golden light is now wrapping around your heart, healing and filling it completely with absolute love. Enjoy this wonderful feeling for as long as you want.

12. Say this affirmation to yourself: "I have a happy, healthy heart and am free to be me now," as you imagine yourself being completely free, happy and healthy.

13. When you are ready, take another deep breath and let go of this image. Slowly begin to walk back along the path on which you came.

14. Count slowly from 1 to 10 and allow your body and mind to become more and more awake with each number. Feel yourself return to the present, and when you open your eyes, feel completely refreshed and alert again. Have a good stretch.

Practise this meditation in full for at least seven days. Soon, you should begin to feel lighter and freer from any negative thoughts and feelings about your previous relationship. Once you know those old feelings are gone, you can do a shorter version of this meditation, skipping steps 7 to 10, and simply enjoy the pleasant walk in nature with the healing sunlight around your heart.

This simple meditation method will form the basis of the future visualisation exercises that I have for you, so it is a good idea to make a habit of practising this one regularly. It should only take a few minutes every day and it will easily become a routine. Very soon, you will notice the benefits of being calmer, more centred and at peace inside yourself.

B. Write it on Paper

One of the best ways to unload your emotions or thoughts is by writing them in a journal. This is not like keeping a diary, nor is it a method of 'journaling', which is usually used for recording events in chronological order. The purpose of this kind of writing is to get your thoughts and feelings out of your head and onto paper. This will relieve your mind so that you no longer need to dwell on them.

Start by getting a separate notebook and keep it strictly private. Do not use the same notebook that you are using for all the other exercises in this book. Also, don't do this on your computer or other electronic device because it won't be as effective as writing on paper.

Start by writing down whatever has been going around your mind recently. Don't worry about remembering things exactly, in the order they happened or trying to figure out why. Just write anything that comes to mind. If you don't know where to begin, start by thinking of the following:

- Your thoughts about your previous relationship. Scribble down some of the the events, issues and everything you experienced. For example, where, when and what he/she did and you did at that time.
- All of your emotions and feelings, good and bad, around that relationship. Express it as much as you can in words.

Be spontaneous, honest and free as you write. Do not spend time trying to make perfect sentences, structuring paragraphs or worrying about your grammar. It does not matter if things are not in sequence or if there are points you forgot. No one is ever going to read this, not even you. So do not look back through it, re-read or correct anything at this stage. Do not stop to analyse anything you have written.

As you get into the habit of writing down all that is on your mind you will, not only release any pent-up emotions but also, feel a sense of freedom and begin to get a clearer understanding of what actually happened. Quite often, people who journal this way will tell you it is a great way to gain clarity, find solutions and make sense of particular experiences they have had. You will start to gain greater insight, self-awareness and a wider perspective, which you might not get by simply thinking about it.

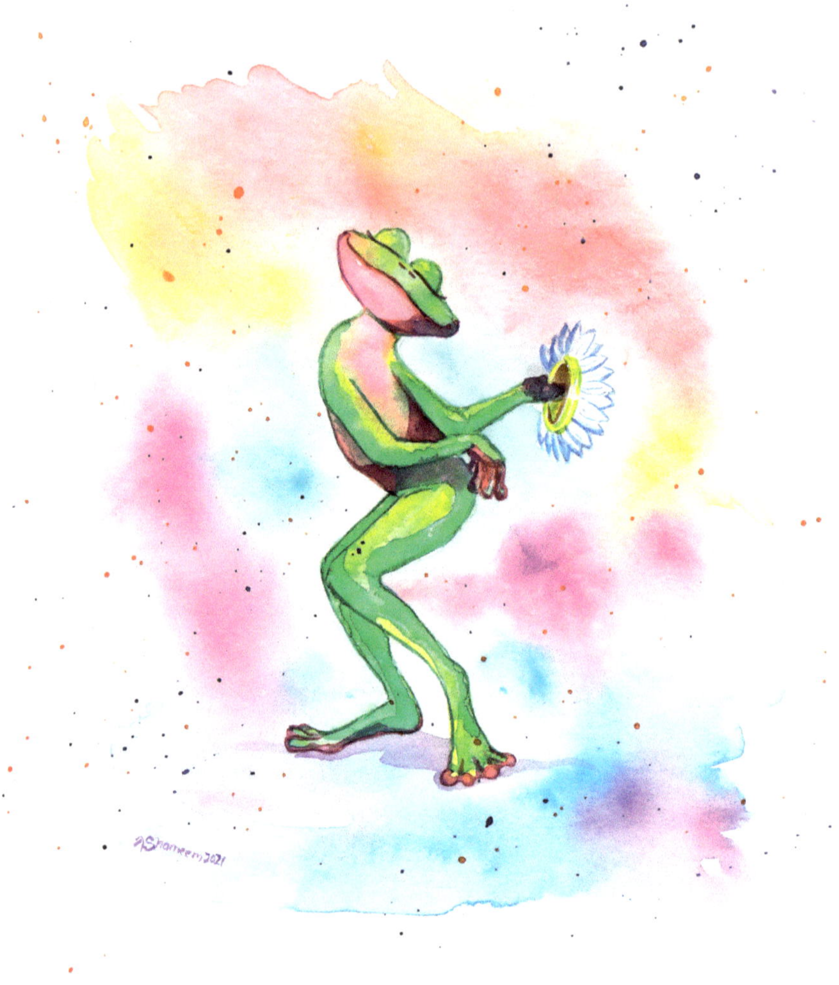

Shameem 2021

5. The Princess Awakens

As the ship sailed into the sunset, she looked back once more toward the shore, feeling a little tug at her heart. This certainly was a great adventure, full of unexpected surprises. Yet the surprise she longed for, seemed far out of reach.

"Don't be so glum, princess," ordered the captain. "Dance and be merry! For thee has much to celebrate."
"But my heart yet longs for something... perhaps the lost treasure," she sighed.
"Why, we have wind in our sails, a full hold and our fiddler to cheer us!" the captain beamed. "Be glad of such tidings for today, we have calm seas. While the 'morrow may bring storms."
"Yes, I suppose," she conceded.
"Aye! There be not many princesses sailing the high seas," the captain continued brightly. "Well now, look at thy feet! They be tapping a rhythm, I see. Now, dance and sing, my dear! Is that not a treasure, indeed?"

Becoming a Princess

Leaving behind my old life and going abroad to work allowed me, not only a sanctuary from the financial difficulties and broken relationship, but also a chance to find my true self and discover the person I never knew I was. Until that point my default programme was to be a nice, positive 'good girl', work hard and take care of others. The possibility that I could do something to make *myself happy* meant stepping into unchartered waters, which I didn't even know that I didn't know.

You see, in my mind, that wedding ceremony was not what I would call a real marriage. It was actually a marriage of convenience, although I didn't realise it at the time. I had already convinced myself that Ted was the right man because we were both artists and he fit my romantic notions of all that I needed in a life partner. Later, I remember listing the reasons in my journal for agreeing to the ceremony: "It's high time. I am 25 years old, that's old enough. We've already invested so much time together. I've gone to all the effort of convincing my parents. And yes, of course, we love each other." I was too naïve to understand that I had been pursuing that relationship for all the wrong reasons.

Before I was sucked down the rabbit hole, Ted and I had already discussed and agreed that first, we would live together and then, later, consider marriage. However, things changed dramatically once I'd revealed to my mother that I had a boyfriend. As expected, there was an almighty explosion at first, but after her fury subsided, she persuaded me to 'do the right thing' according to our culture. I gave in, thinking that if marriage was on the cards anyway, then it might as well be now. After all, I wanted to keep the peace and please my parents.

However, there was also a hidden incentive. I knew that by going ahead with the marriage, I would gain a long-awaited bonus prize: it would be my ticket to gaining my freedom.

This may sound rather absurd in our modern world but at that time, according to Bangladeshi culture, a young woman must be kept 'protected' by her parents or guardians until she is 'married off'. This meant that I was not allowed to do many of the things that my friends took for granted. Whilst at school, there was no staying out after dark or overnight with friends. Even after the age of eighteen, I couldn't go to a pub or nightclub where alcohol and socialising were involved. I certainly wasn't allowed to go away on holiday with a female friend, even when I was in my early twenties.

Moreover, the culture made a young woman feel as though she was not of any significance until she got married and had a husband and children. Luckily, unlike some Muslim parents, my parents were not extremely strict and I was allowed to go to the odd *birthday* party in the evening or on school field trips for 'educational' purposes, of course. They naïvely assumed that we were always chaperoned or supervised by teachers and parents at these events. Little did they know..!

Upon finishing school, it was expected that I should go to university but the idea that I might have to live away from home was something that never occurred to my parents. After failing to get into any of the highest-ranking London-based art colleges, as my father had wanted, I was offered one of the few remaining places left in the country. It was at an unknown small art and design college that, much to my mother's horror, was based in a town situated more than a hundred miles away from home. But I pleaded with my parents and insisted on going. I was nineteen and desperate to flee the nest.

Despite my father's best intentions to have me board near the college with a local Asian family, who were supposedly watching over me, there was little they could do to hold me down. Within a few weeks, I had made new friends, was going out as often as I liked and loving every minute of my newfound freedom. Being at art college felt liberating as I found that all the other students were equally odd and non-conformist too. I was no longer made to feel awkward and nerdy but equal to everyone else there. My new environment was perfect and at last, I fitted in and *had* a social life.

The ugly frogling soon shed several layers of insecurity, leapt happily into her new princess role, pulling on her crown and donning some pretty frocks to match. Of course, no one had warned the princess about her newfound charm and that it might enchant every frog, toad and newt in the local pond. Her beliefs about being unattractive and unlikeable soon crumbled away as she discovered the art of how to attract men. It seemed, all she had to do was simply be her natural, sunny, funny self. She realised that she had a hidden talent for making people laugh, which had an added bonus: it made for excellent bait – how extraordinary!

I started off not knowing a thing about men or what they might actually want. But after just a few trips and bumps, my eyes opened and I quickly learned about male motivations and how to manage them. Luckily, my college buddies were mainly male, and being the only girl in the gang, they would all kindly look out for me in case of any undesirable attention.

Once, I remember being at a house party, and whilst one guy was trying to gain my interest, out of the corner of my eye, across the room, I saw an argument starting to brew between Sam, my tall skinny boyfriend, and Mick, my college mate, who was equally tall and skinny. They both seemed quite inebriated and were getting into a heated debate. Then, before I knew it, there was a shove, a lunge, and a sudden frenzy of long arms and legs flailing at each other! No sooner, some of the other guys jumped in and immediately pulled them apart.

Luckily, only their egos were a little bruised and no one was hurt. I had no idea why they were squabbling because the two would usually, get along fine. A short time later, I found myself sitting on the floor, leaning against the wall and soothing them both, one either side of me, with their heads on my shoulders. Eventually, they laughed about it, apologised and shook hands with each other.

When I probed a little, they whispered their drunken confessions in my ear and I discovered that they were fighting over me! I was amused, thinking how surreal this scenario was, like a sketch in a romantic comedy. I felt like Scarlett O'Hara from 'Gone with the Wind' in one of the early scenes where she is surrounded by her many admirers at a garden party.[7]

All this attention was doing wonders for her self-confidence and her ego swelled with inflated pride. Within a year of being away from home, the pendulum had truly swung in the opposite direction. The princess was revelling in this newfound, forbidden treasure and soaked up all the male attention that came her way.

*Alas, upon returning to her family home two years later, she found herself having to abide by her parents' old fashioned, irritating restrictions yet again. It would be impossible to have the kind of freedom, to which she had since grown accustomed, whilst living with them. The **party** princess would have to knuckle down, work hard and think of a new plan.*

Staying at my parents was stifling so I quickly got my first full-time job, started earning and paid for my own driving lessons. As soon as I'd passed the test and got my licence, I bought my own car; this was my ticket to freedom. In just over 18 months, I had steadily progressed to my third job and was working in London. It was just far enough away that I would not have to live at home.

Although I had moved out, I didn't gain any genuine independence from the cultural restrictions until I was married. All those rules that had bound me since childhood fell away, quite literally, overnight as I became, no more the responsibility of my parents, but that of my new husband. At last, I could be an adult, be free to make my own decisions and do as *I* wanted. But, of course, living with Ted did not turn out to be the joyful, easy happy-ever-after of my dreams. That relationship took me back to 'frogland', drowned my party spirit and replaced it with drudgery. That is when I first found myself sinking down into the murky, muddy depths of despair and self-doubt.

Genuine Freedom

Having arrived on the cruise ship, it was time to shed some more layers and experience freedom on a whole new level. The big wide world was waiting to be conquered. I found myself amongst many different people from all over the world and in a strange, new environment. I was swept up on a wave of curiosity and exciting, new encounters. Being in unfamiliar territory was not at all uncomfortable as life had prepared me well. Whether in social situations or at work, I had often been the odd one, the foreigner and I always had to find a way to fit in.

In comparison to college, this was far more liberating as no one on board pried into anything personal other than asking about where you were from. There were multitudes of multi-national people all working together and all speaking English but with a wonderful array of accents but which, didn't matter at all because we were all aliens. I was delighted that I didn't have to explain or think about how to behave, act or speak in order to be accepted. It was truly refreshing as there was no pressure from any family, colleagues, culture or society upon me.

Despite the ship's strict rules and regulations for crew members, I felt freer than I had ever been before, and for the first time in my life, I could just be *me*. Other than having fun, as a 'newbie', I still had much to learn. For instance, if we were caught breaking the rules or being in the wrong place at the wrong time, we could easily get a warning. If we got three warnings, we could lose our jobs and be sent home. So, I smiled sweetly, followed instructions, did my job and stayed away from trouble.

This exciting new world allowed me the perfect environment to stop focusing on all my personal problems, the struggles that I had left behind back home, and just be myself in the here and now. When it came to my free time, I found myself growing a strange but wonderful new attitude. I was learning to ask myself, "What do *I want* to do? and, "What do I *feel* like doing?" It had never occurred to me before then, that I might have a choice or could put myself first because all I had ever done was what I *thought* others expected of me. And so, it slowly began to dawn on me that I really had no clue about *who* I was or what *I* really felt, thought or believed in.

It was an incredible awakening as I became more conscious of the real me. I began to celebrate the happy, joyful, confident, easy-going me who had just begun to blossom whilst at college, but which had then been halted as soon as I had returned home. My true spirit had been, quite literally, not allowed out to play and stifled since childhood. Now, at last, I could go out, be free and do as *I* wanted. So, I would take every opportunity to explore, go on tours, see new places and spend time taking in the many different cultures surrounding me.

I began to realise just how important travel was for me. I loved visiting new countries and learning how other people live and think. My European and North American counterparts that made up the majority of 'staff' who worked on the upper decks, in the casino, shops and entertainment departments, tended to keep to themselves. Meanwhile, you would often find me downstairs on the lower decks, hanging around with the 'crew' who were from many other parts of the world such as the Caribbean islands, Latin American countries, the Philippines, China, India, etc.

I don't believe that my colleagues upstairs were actually being prejudiced but rather that they didn't know how to mix with different cultures. On board, there was also a hierarchical segregation of officers, staff and crew, which didn't help to break the boundaries either. The crew downstairs were mostly men and did all the hard labour; the cleaning, cooking, engineering, maintenance and serving in the restaurants and bars. It bothered me that they worked much longer hours, toiled below decks where there were few windows and were never allowed to mingle with the passengers on the upper decks. So, I treated them as equals and with the same respect as anyone else. They soon accepted me as one of their own and I became a familiar face in the crew mess.

As my interest in their ways grew, I slowly became aware that I had a deep love of all things Latin; the people, the food, the Spanish language, music, and of course, dancing. Any kind of music with a beat would usually get me up dancing but, for some strange reason, Latin music and dance seemed to feed my soul. Until then, I didn't know just how hungry I was to dance. It was a part of me that had never been allowed to fully express itself in my earlier years. Not even after marriage, as Ted didn't like going to nightclubs or listening to dance music. But now, I was free to dance whenever the rhythm moved me. I could visit the onboard disco until curfew, then head down to the crew bar for more music until the early hours. Whenever we were in port, we would also frequent the numerous bars and clubs nearby.

I remember being on board only a few weeks when I was invited to my first 'crew party' by my workmates, Jenny and Kate. "You've got to come! It's for Jamaican Independence Day. Crew parties are always loads of fun," they said cheerfully. "There's usually music and delicious Caribbean food; jerk chicken – yum!"

Well, of course, I was not going to say no to a party! That evening, as soon we'd finished work, I changed into something more comfortable and enthusiastically followed the girls. As we were now no longer in our uniforms, we were not allowed to be seen in any of the passenger areas. So, we had to take a long detour; through a maze of corridors across the lower decks, down steps, along gangways and past the engine rooms to finally arrive at our destination on the 'rope deck', situated at the bow or front of the ship.

By the time we arrived, the party was in full swing, the reggae music was pumping out of huge speakers and the place was filled with mostly Caribbean men. They were happily letting their hair down as there were no officers around to dampen the atmosphere. Alas, we were there too late and the food had already run out; the jerk chicken and rice and peas were all gone. All that was left were the big drums of punch, which I happily helped myself to.

Whilst I was getting into the music and bobbing to the beat, Jenny and Kate decided it was not their thing. They had missed the food and weren't very keen on the music and so, they left fairly soon after arriving. It seemed to me that the girls – my white European and American colleagues – felt somewhat intimidated by the all-male black Caribbean crowd. But it didn't bother me at all where these guys were from or what they might look like. I was used to being the only girl in such environments and anyway, the music was great! To me it meant peace, love and *'everytin' irie'* and so, I happily continued soaking up the Jamaican vibes, *'whinin'* my body to the reggae rhythms. And for once, the guys didn't pay much attention to me.

Before long, I began to feel a quite dizzy and tired. I later learned that what had tasted like innocent fruit punch was actually made with generous quantities of '151' rum which apparently is 75% alcohol! You could say it had some serious punch! "I'd better go home to bed," I decided. "If I don't, I'll fall asleep right here on a pile of ropes". I started to make my way aft, heading towards the back of the ship, where the crew cabins were located. My head spun and my legs wobbled as I tried to steady myself against the ship's sway. It was especially unnerving climbing back up the stepladders and I remember gripping tightly to the handrails as I edged along the narrow gangways. But somehow, I got through the underground maze without getting lost and eventually made it back. To this day, I still wonder how I managed to navigate the whole way, on my own, considering the state I was in!

Finally, I tiptoed back into my cabin as quietly as possible, trying not to disturb my sleeping roommate, Angie. Luckily, she continued to snore as I brushed my teeth, washed and changed into my nightshirt. Then, very carefully, I climbed the short ladder to my bunk, still swaying and slumped down with great relief. At last, I could just roll into a blissful sleep. But no, my belly had other ideas. The ship's motion made my stomach lurch and my head swirl even more. Normally, the motion of the ocean would rock me to sleep but now it was making me feel quite nauseas.

Alas, my poor, inexperienced stomach and small frame could not cope with such strong alcohol and it didn't want to stay down. I was not afraid of having to vomit but more worried about how I would heave my drowsy body out of my bunk and climb down the ladder again without falling or waking Angie. Another sway of the ship and I knew I had little choice. Somehow, I managed to hoist myself up and clamber down to the bathroom just in time! Angie, thank goodness, slept through the entire ordeal.

Most Valuable Treasure

Our greatest lessons, romantic or otherwise, are usually learned the hard way. I know that many of us can relate to my rum punch story from our own youth. As you can guess, it was not something I repeated ever again. Apart from learning to be more careful about the limits of my physical body, I also began to recognise my inner character and appreciate my deeper needs and desires. Apart from the amazing social life on board, we had to be on our feet for many hours and work some very long days. Hence, I learned that if I were to be professional at work, as well as have fun and go dancing in the evenings, I needed to give myself 'me time'. As I mentioned in the previous chapter, it was essential to create a balance in order to maintain my equilibrium; to be alone, reflect and hear myself think.

As a child, I started out with absolutely zero self-confidence and had no idea what 'self-love' was. Being happy in my own skin or learning to like myself was completely beyond my conception as I was growing up. Despite all the male attention, becoming the party princess and cultivating a façade of outer confidence, I was still far from knowing and embodying genuine self-love. Underneath it all, I was still very insecure and self-critical. The default programme of 'I am not enough' was deeply ingrained and would continue to run for many years to come.

The environment within most of our cultures and societies reinforce the idea that it is 'immodest' to 'bang your own drum' or show that you love yourself. It seems that it is much more acceptable to do the opposite, to belittle oneself and be self-deprecating. I always found that making fun of myself was readily welcomed and appreciated. It was not until I reached my late thirties that I began to understand the meaning of self-respect and how to treat myself well. In other words, that I should treat myself with as much consideration, kindness and value as I would anyone else.

I have since learned many lessons about the art of self-love, which has given me a much healthier foundation for building better, more loving relationships, not only with myself, but also with those I care about. I shed many layers of frog-like beliefs and eventually turned that low self-worth mentality into the genuinely confident woman I have now become. Today, I can happily say I have reached a level of self-esteem that is very secure, stable and resilient. It is far, far removed from that young, naïve, overinflated ego that I once entertained in my early twenties.

Here are some of the insights I gathered along the way, which you might find useful to consider:

- It is really okay to make mistakes. It is okay to get things wrong or make a fool of myself.
- Once you've learned the lesson, let it go. There is no need to continue beating yourself up.
- It doesn't matter if they misunderstand you or what they think of you.
- Those that know the true *you*, love you anyway, just as you are.
- You don't need to keep trying to prove you are right.
- You don't need to prove anything to anyone.

- You gain integrity and self-confidence when you keep your word, no matter if you are right or wrong. Always do as you say you will.
- Your intention and integrity in all that you say and do are paramount.
- Love your body just as it is. Your curves, shape, size and colour are exactly as nature intended.
- Your intelligence, personality, humour, spirit and loving heart are, by far, your greatest assets.
- Gossip or making fun of others is a reflection of your own low self-worth.
- Self-deprecating jokes are unnecessary. You can make people laugh without belittling yourself.
- Talking incessantly and laughing overly loud are indicators of low self-worth.
- Being afraid to speak up and holding back your truth are also indicators of low self-worth.
- If you expect respect from others, you must first, respect yourself.
- Showing emotions and being vulnerable is courageous.
- When you are in company, you don't need to be *doing* anything to be worthy and loveable.

One of the most important keys to having a lasting, happy relationship with another person is to recognise the *'who'* you truly are and secondly, to *fall in love* with *all* that you are. In other words, accepting and enjoying your whole, authentic self is essential for healing your heart, mind and spirit. It is only when you can fully appreciate yourself that you attract the kind of relationship in which you will be fully appreciated by another. Why? Because you cannot expect another person to fall in love with who you are – the true you – if you cannot do so yourself. You must recognise, acknowledge and accept yourself first. Yes, I know, this is much easier said than done!

If you want to increase your self-worth and self-love, you must first get to know the whole of you under all the layers. We need to uncover who you are beneath the outer layers and the default programmes which were installed by your environment, social, cultural and familial expectations and beliefs. However, the good news is that finding your real, true, authentic self does not need to be as tough for you as it was for me.

You certainly won't need to pack up your life and go travelling for several years in order to find yourself. (Although, if you can, I highly recommend travelling as it is an incredible education in itself.) You can stay at home, right where you are, and find your authentic self by using the tools I have given in the following Lesson. To unwrap the many layers that make up your whole persona, you will need a little time, patience and thinking. Eventually, you will understand the real WHO you are, which includes all of your wants, needs, traits, core values, quirks, warts and all.

LESSON 4: Know Thyself

A. Recognise Your Whole Self

This exercise will help you identify the many elements that make up your unique self. Take your time to acknowledge every aspect of yourself as you do this.

Figure 2. The Onion Analogy

1. Imagine you are made up of many layers like an onion. In your notebook, draw a similar diagram as big as possible, taking up the whole page, as shown in Figure 2.
2. Entitle each of the concentric circles with the headings; Body, Personality, Mind, Spirit.

3. Each circle represents different aspects of everything that makes up who you are. Inside each circle, write as many words that come to mind which describe the following characteristics:
   - **Body**: your physical self; face, hair, skin, body, gender and outer appearance. This is you at surface level and it is what other people see at first glance.
   - **Personality**: these are your personality traits that refer to how you speak, act and behave. It is the external expression of yourself which can be observed by others.
   - **Mind**: this aspect refers to your thoughts, feelings and inner nature. It is about your thought processes and internal emotions that others usually do not see.
   - **Spirit**: this is your core self, made up of your personal values and deepest beliefs. These are the ideals and principles by which you conduct your life and that underlie your motivations. Your core beliefs are what you know to be your truth. No one can observe these but sometimes, they are indicated through your actions.

For most of us, the characteristics about the Body, and some of the Personality, will probably change as we get older. However, your inner self, the Mind characteristics, are less likely to change over time.

It is your deepest, core self, your Spirit that rarely changes. Most people continue to hold the same core values and these deep beliefs remain the same throughout their entire lives.

Hence, when you become aware of your core self, you will appreciate your authentic nature more as it is this part of you that makes up the *'WHO'* you truly are.

To help with your onion diagram, Figure 3 shows two tables with lists of characteristics from which you can select. They refer to the Personality, Mind and Spirit aspects. Of course, these lists are not comprehensive, but they will help you to start thinking about your own characteristics. Most probably, you will find many other words to describe yourself.

You will notice that some of the words are interchangeable between aspects and appear in both lists. Feel free to be flexible and adapt the words you feel best describe you. You might choose to overlap certain words between the circles.

Figure 3. Lists of Characteristics

Personality or Mind							
Adaptable	Decisive	Generous	Likeable	Proactive	Shy
Adventurous	Dedicated	Gentle	Loyal	Punctual	Sincere
Angry	Dependable	Gregarious	Meticulous	Quiet	Sociable
Authoritative	Determined	Helpful	Motivated	Rational	Stable
Calm	Direct	Honest	Organised	Relaxed	Stressful
Caring	Discerning	Humorous	Outgoing	Reliable	Stubborn
Compassionate	Disciplined	Imaginative	Patient	Reserved	Thorough
Confident	Empathetic	Independent	Perceptive	Resourceful	Tolerant
Conscientious	Excitable	Innovative	Persevering	Respectful	Tough
Considerate	Fastidious	Intuitive	Persuasive	Sad	Trusting
Cooperative	Firm	Joyous	Pragmatic	Sensitive	Wise
Creative	Flexible	Leader	Precise	Scattered	Worrisome

Spirit					
Achievement	Competitive	Fun	Leadership	Practical	Stability
Active	Creative	Harmony	Learning	Predictable	Status
Adaptable	Culture	Happiness	Leisure	Progressive	Structure
Ambition	Develop	Healthy	Location	Promotion	Supportive
Alternative	Discover	Helping others	Loving	Rational	Teaching
Autonomy	Ethical	High income	Marriage	Recognition	Timely
Balance	Excitement	Honesty	Material	Religion	Tolerance
Benefit	Evolve	Independence	Modern	Respect	Tradition
Busy	Fame	Individuality	Moral	Risk	Trust
Career	Family	Influence	Organised	Security	Truth
Caring	Fitness	Innovative	Passion	Service	Variety
Challenge	Freedom	Joy	Physical	Singular	Wealth
Community	Friendships	Knowledge	Political	Society	Wisdom

Remember that there are no good or bad characteristics here. It is more about how you interpret them and see them in yourself. When you have completed your onion diagram, you may become aware of certain qualities that you might not be happy with and would like to change. Recognising precisely what you want to change is the biggest step in transforming any aspect of your life.

B. Mirror Exercise

Now that you have a good, clear understanding of all that makes up your unique self, the next step is to fall in love with every part of yourself. Here is one method that has been proven to work and which I have adapted slightly for our purposes.[8] This exercise should only take about five minutes. Do this every morning and/or evening for a minimum of 30 days.

1. Stand in front of your mirror. Most people use their bathroom mirror as it is in a private place. Take a deep breath and put aside any other thoughts for a few minutes.
2. Bring to mind any characteristics about yourself which you usually tend to be critical of. Consider how these parts of you actually serve and benefit you. Now, instead, create positive, alternative words to describe each of them (e.g., "I love my thighs because they are strong, function perfectly and allow me to walk, run, sit and cuddle my children on my lap").
3. Now, look deep into your own eyes and say any of the following affirmations out loud and with feeling. Choose at least three or four of these and fill in the blanks with your own words from your onion diagram.
   - I love you just the way you are.
   - You are more than enough.
   - I love your… because… (from your Body)
   - I am proud that you are… because… (from your Personality traits)
   - I am glad that you are… because… (from your Mind and mental traits)
   - You are accomplished, beautiful, clever, courageous, generous, kind, talented, wise, etc. (Use whatever positive adjectives you like.)
   - You deserve to be loved and you are loveable.
   - I am so grateful that you love and take care of me every day.
4. When you become more comfortable with doing this exercise, you can replace the words 'You are' with 'I am' and 'your' with 'my'. These statements are 'positive affirmations', which we will discuss in more detail later.

The first time you do this mirror exercise, it may feel silly, awkward or fake or you may even find yourself getting emotional. After a few days, it will become easier and you will start to notice a change in your ability to say the words.

The first time I did the mirror exercise, I was quite resistant and it was very difficult for me. I could not even look into my own eyes without crying. It was as though I was tapping into some deeper layers, which did not want to be uncovered but that desperately needed healing. However, those initial barriers disintegrated very quickly and I soon found many more positive attributes about myself to affirm every day.

Becoming more aware of yourself is one of the most important factors to becoming truly content with being you. As you learn to identify and acknowledge your body, face, personality, moods, beliefs, attitudes, words, ideas, choices, and so on, you will become more accepting of yourself. Then, as you take stock of all the little things that make up your complex and distinct persona, you will recognise and appreciate your authentic, true self more readily. In turn, you will become less self-critical or concerned about what others might think and stop trying to conform to their expectations.

When you are fully in tune with exactly who you are and appreciate yourself more, you will also find that you make better decisions as you will be more discerning about your own particular needs. For instance, you will choose the people, activities and environments that suit you better, as well as the kind of person you want to have as your life partner. Whether they are good or bad traits, you can be more honest and upfront about what you will or won't bring to a relationship.

Genuine self-love means learning to see, accept and love all of your unique self as completely as possible. It is an art that takes time to perfect and, which is never a hundred percent perfect. You will need to be patient and compassionate with yourself, especially during the early stages of the process. Very soon, you will start to notice a shift in your mindset, the way you feel inside and how you treat yourself. By doing the above exercises, you will slowly heal your heart, mind and spirit on a deeper level for the long term. Thereafter, not only will you grow your level of self-worth, but also cause a positive ripple effect upon all those around you. You will probably hear people commenting on how you are looking happier and more radiant. If so, please do write to me as I would love to hear your story and how you've grown

In my eBook *Am I Happy with Myself?* you can learn more ways to increase your self-love and turn your inner confidence into rock-solid, unshakeable self-esteem.

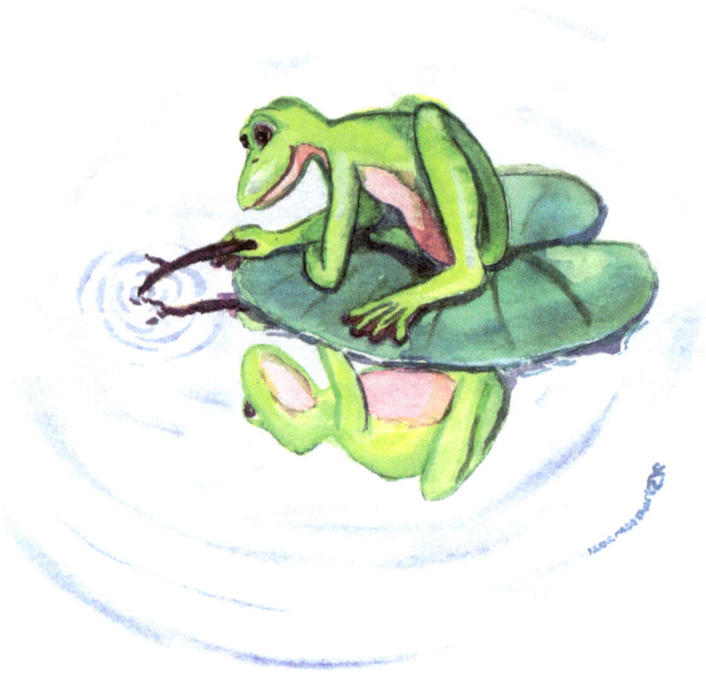

6. Tuning into Magic

After many weary journeys, the princess returned home with an empty heart and empty-handed. The treasure she sought was nowhere to be found.

"My one true love, oh, you must exist out there somewhere?" She sighed as she sat by the pond at the bottom of her garden gazing down into water. Poking a stick into the water, she half hoped that a frog might leap out and magically turn into her prince.

"Why, of course, he exists," replied a low voice from the sky, startling the princess. Looking up, she was met by two large blinking eyes. There, in the tree above her, sat an old owl.
"But you must first learn to use your magic wand," continued the owl.
"Who are you?" asked the princess, confused. "And what wand?"
"Well, that one, obviously," replied the owl, pointing at her stick.

Peter Pan

It seemed like an age had passed since leaving Ted and a whole new life was unfolding for me. I was back from my travels and living on dry land again. Luckily, I soon acquired a steady job, which I really enjoyed, and my own place to live. Although I missed the sunshine and sea, it was good to be me again and do the work I was doing. I began to feel ready to open the door again for a better, happier, healthier relationship.

Using the visualisation method (which I will explain more about later), I had set an intention to attract only the right kind of man; someone who would be fun, positive and truly appreciate me. He would not only be sweet and caring towards me but also have his own home, a good job and be self-sufficient. As you can guess, the reason was because, until then, my experience with men had always been the opposite; men who could not support themselves financially or value me.

Then, lo and behold, the genie appeared and granted the princess exactly that which she had wished for! Within a matter of months, she met a lovely man in a London dance club who turned out to be all that she had wanted. "This is it! At last, I've manifested the right One!" She thought ecstatically and began to dream of her happy-ever-after. This time, the princess had indeed stepped into a real fairy tale Neverland and would learn how to fly. Only, the wings were not quite as she had first imagined.

Dan was tall, dark-haired, a little shy and a couple of years older than me. He was self-employed and owned a delightful little cottage. I instantly fell for his boyish smile, quirky humour and kind, big-hearted nature. He always insisted on paying for everything whenever we went out which was a pleasant surprise and something I was really not used to. "Keep your hard-earned pennies," he would say with a smile. "I make six times what you do," and he would gently push away my hand holding out my purse.

Being with Dan was a joyous breath of fresh air. At last, I had met a 'good guy'. There were hardly any disagreements between us. Instead, there was much silliness, fun and laughter. Very soon, we both fell happily in love with each other. He generously shared all his little luxuries with me, which was more than I had ever hoped for. We saw theatre shows, went on holidays and dined at good restaurants together. It was all very novel to me and made me feel very special. If we went to a nightclub, he would let me do my thing and dance for as long as I liked whilst staying in the background, smiling and keeping a protective eye over me. At last, this was a relationship that made me feel safe, secure and loved.

As we got to know each other, I told him of my past, family issues, travels, hopes and dreams. He would always listen to my stories with childlike curiosity. And just like a child, his eyes would glaze over whenever I spoke of my deeper thoughts about cultural issues, spiritual aspirations or psychological theories. I couldn't quite tell whether it was because he couldn't grasp the ideas or if he was simply not interested. My need for any intellectual or serious conversation was usually pushed aside for jovial, mindless banter.

After a year or so, I became increasingly frustrated that the relationship was going nowhere. I was still longing to be married and have at least one child. At thirty years old, I thought it was high time for me to experience motherhood. He, on the other hand, did not want to talk of the future and preferred to continue enjoying, what he called a 'Peter Pan' life-style for as long as possible. "Settle down and grow up?! Whatever for?" he would baulk, whenever I raised the subject.

You see, herein lay my lesson: I needed to learn to be more careful about what I wished for. I had wanted someone to simply love me, have fun with and who would be financially comfortable. I forgot to add that we should also be compatible in our thinking; psychologically and emotionally, and especially, our needs and wishes for the future.

Interestingly, whilst I was hankering after a life that was the 'norm', the gods had other plans for me. One weekend, I went to visit Nicky, my dear friend whom I used to work with on the ships. She also returned to England around the same time as I had, and soon after, met a man from her home town and got married. They were now settled in a wonderful home, and recently, she had given birth to a beautiful, healthy baby boy.

I sat on the sofa in her living room, holding the joyful, gurgling babe on my lap. "I am so, so happy for you! You're incredibly lucky, Nick," I said, gesturing to the huge house, baby and everything she seemed to have. "You had your fair share of frogs in the past, I know! And now look at you – you've got your prince and perfect happy-ever-after fairy tale." She smiled and simply said, "I guess so", with a look of empathy.

"This is all I really want," I continued as I hugged and burbled at her son. "I don't care about a career. Well, perhaps one day, I will go back to college and get that degree but it's not really that important to me right now."
"What degree is that?" enquired Nicky. I went on to explain how I had flunked Art College years ago because I had suffered a terrible broken heart and that one day, I hoped to return to my studies. Perhaps, when I am much older, married and the children have all grown up. Getting a degree was a goal I had always had, since childhood, but never managed to achieve, despite several attempts to get back into Art College over the years. I also told her about all my concerns with Dan and our relationship as it seemed we wanted different things for our future.

After listening intently, Nicky took her bouncing boy from my arms, sniffed his behind and laid him down on his changing mat on the floor. I watched as her hands deftly unpacked, cleaned his bottom and repackaged him neatly whilst maintaining a constant cooing chatter with her delighted son. I wondered if I would be any good at changing a baby as I couldn't remember the last time I had done so. It was certainly not a pleasant task, I decided, trying to hide a grimace with a smile.

"Why wait to go back to college?" Nicky said eventually. "I'm telling you, motherhood may seem amazing, and it is, but don't kid yourself – it aint all that great. Why wait all those years? Why put your dreams on the shelf, waiting for children that may or may not arrive?" She paused to test the bottle she had prepared, then placed it in the baby's mouth and continued, "I mean, you could do it now in the meantime, whilst waiting for your man to do the right thing. Even if you do get married and have kids, well, I'm sure you'll find a way around it."

She had a point. It was something I hadn't given any serious thought to. During the long drive home, I found myself engrossed in thought as I started to question and re-think my life's plans. "What have I done with my life so far? I mean, really, what have I actually accomplished until now? Hmm... nothing much," I concluded. Whilst I'd been focusing on trying to find Mr Right, the years had been slipping me by.

After all, if this relationship with Dan was going nowhere, and I wasn't getting what I really wanted with him, maybe Nicky was right. "Maybe I should be making better use of my time. Could I spend my life with someone without ever getting married or having kids? Or could I have kids outside of marriage? Should I even be thinking of having kids with someone who doesn't want them? Will we stay together? What if we don't? Would I consider having a child alone? With or without kids, what if, in the end, I stay single forever? Would that be such a disaster?

In which case, what would I want to say I have done with my life?" These and many other questions came up for analysis and started swirling around my head.

I spent several nights lying awake, trying to decide my future. Slowly but surely, I faced the truth of my deeper feelings and the long-held idea of motherhood soon began to loosen its grip. All this re-evaluation led to a much more important question, the answer to which would steer the course of my life: "What do *I really want* to achieve in my life? When I am very old and coming to the end of my life, what legacy do I want to say I have left behind?"

A New Direction

I had come to a major turning point, and as usual, I turned to my 'Fairy Godmother' for guidance (aka Fae). She is usually the wisest soul I know and the only one that I can always rely upon to give me straight answers. Who is this Fae, I hear you ask? Be patient – I shall reveal all very soon!

So, after much deliberating, pondering and talking with Fae, it became clear that I should, not only return to study, but change my career direction completely. Until then, I had always assumed that art, design and graphics were my forte. However, upon deeper inspection of my interests, skills, aptitudes and *who* I truly am, I discovered that I had a strong leaning toward psychology. It was the subject that had always fascinated me and even whilst at Art College, I was drawn to books on Freud, Jung and self-development in the library. I began to realise that I had always been very interested in looking at human behaviour, attitudes and expression, even in my art work.

All at once, the jigsaw puzzle pieces were falling into place! I decided to take the huge leap, return to university and take a degree in psychology. However, the careers service advised me that if so, I would need to take another one or two years of preliminary studies, including A-level psychology, in order to gain the right qualifications and appropriate 'credits' for entrance to University. This was not good news and I certainly couldn't afford five or more years of full-time study. In fact, at that time, I had no idea how I was going to fund myself through college again.

However, Fae had better ideas and suggested I should just go ahead and make an application that year – in fact, as soon as possible – for the degree course without bothering with all the preliminary courses. After all, what had I to lose? At worst, I might get a refusal, which was something that I was already quite used to, and could try again next year, if I decide to go down the conventional path.

I decided to discuss my idea with a friendly colleague, a student advisor, whom I could trust to keep things confidential. She suggested that there might be an alternative route that might just work. I could complete my NVQ (a vocational qualification), which I had been dawdling with for over two years, and it would technically give me the right number of credits. So, I quickly set about preparing my university application and getting my boring NVQ finished.

My first choice of university was within driving distance, and if I could get a place there, I would be absolutely delighted as it would mean not having to move farther away. However, given my track record with previous university applications, I wasn't going to get my hopes up. This time, I would just take it easy, not worry and accept whatever happens. I decided not to get stressed about anything but just to give it my best shot. If it didn't work out, there was nothing to lose, my boss wouldn't need to know and I could continue with my job.

Hence, I didn't get too excited when I received an invitation to the open day which included an initial interview for 'mature' students. Surely, this was just standard practice, probably to see if we understood the application process and fitted their selection criteria, I thought. So, when I arrived at the Psychology department, I wasn't at all stressed but just curious and calm. Although, I did feel a little conspicuous as I had arrived straight from work and was still wearing my smart office suit whilst others were dressed quite casually. As it was almost the end of the open day, most of the visiting students had already been and gone. I looked around wondering if I had missed everything.

"Excuse me, could you possibly tell me where I might find the applications administrator?" I asked a scraggly-looking professor type with long white hair.
"Whom shall I say is asking?" he answered, peering over his glasses. I introduced myself and showed him the letter of invitation which I had received from the university.

He seemed to smirk as he looked me up and down and replied, "Well, then, in that case, it is I you need to see," as if making fun of my accent. I had expected to find a secretarial-type person but I later discovered that as well as being the 'administrator' for new entrants, his actual role was, indeed, the professor of 'Biological Psychology'.

He then led me into a small study room for 'a chat'. I sat down and wondered if this would be just a briefing before the actual interview. I waited for him to begin, as he seemed quite unprepared, and eventually started rambling on about the university and courses offered. I listened politely and waited to hear something I didn't know. Of course, I had done my homework and read the college prospectus, which explained all that he was trying to tell me. I waited for some difficult questions but none transpired. However, the twinkle in his eyes gave away what was actually on his mind and so, whilst pretending not to notice, I decided to take full advantage of the circumstances.

I turned up my business-like charm, asked pertinent questions and gently steered the interview towards a positive response from him. It was a technique I'd learned whilst working in recruitment many years before. It seemed he was rather amused by my manner and only asked me a few questions about how I might be able to afford to study if I gave up my job. I smiled, evading the question and answered confidently, "I think I can manage my own finances, thank you. It's not something the university need be concerned with".

However, I was more concerned about whether I would get a place at all, given my current number of credits, so I explained the details of my previous qualifications. He quietly listened and eventually said, "No problem, but I cannot offer you an unconditional place as you don't have the required credits yet. So… we'll offer you a conditional place. That means it is on condition that you pass your NVQ." He didn't need to spell it out. I understood perfectly what a conditional place meant.

Afterwards, as I walked back to the car park, I was still in disbelief. I ran through the discussion again, repeating the words he'd said in my head and digesting their meaning. "Am I really in?" Then, the reality sunk in as to what had just happened. I was overjoyed! I punched the air with excitement. "YES, I'M IN!" I squealed out loud. "Oh, my goodness, I just got myself accepted into next year's course! Wow, I got it!" I was utterly overjoyed, and my head started to spin with all the things I'd have to do next.

"How the heck did that happen?!" I was completely amazed at how I had managed to get a place, at my first choice of university, without having to do any extra study. According to the careers advisor, I did not stand a chance because I had never studied psychology before and my only qualifications were art and design A-levels from school. Remembering just how tough the application process was for art colleges, this process had turned out to be incredibly easy.

Completing and passing my NVQ would be a doddle as I only had to finish writing up the coursework. So now, my place was practically guaranteed! I was totally elated and felt extremely grateful. The visualisations had truly worked and I had manifested my seat at university! Fae was right; all I had to do was give it a try.

Now, my life was about to move in a completely different and unplanned direction. Everything falling into place so easily was definitely a good sign. It meant that I was finally on the right path. This was a perfect example of how life becomes easier and coincidental things happen to work in your favour, when you become aligned with your real life purpose.

As for Dan and I, well, you can guess what happened. Within a year, the relationship sadly ended as I faced my inner truth. He was a wonderful man but I could not expect something from him that he simply couldn't give. Eventually, I also came to the conclusion that marriage and kids had become secondary for me. They would be nice but not absolutely necessary for my true happiness. What I wanted more than anything was to have a good, solid relationship with someone who truly understood me and that I could really talk with. Alas, Dan was not *the one* and we soon went our separate ways, both equally broken-hearted.

The dream of finding Mr Right, getting married and having kids was not forgotten but carefully wrapped up and placed on the shelf. Whilst the door to my heart remained slightly ajar, I focused my attention on achieving a much yearned for life goal. At first, the 'lab report' assignments seemed like arduous, perplexing tasks to me and I had to hike up a steep learning curve, especially during the first semester. I was not naturally inclined to being *academic* and the rigid practices and protocols were quite outside of my comfort zone. Scientific study methods take the very opposite approach to studying art and design. One does not score points for being creative, certainly not at beginner's level, and thus, my mindset had to turn 180º in order to conform to the standards required.

Finally, after four long years, I attained not just my graduate degree but also successfully completed a master's degree. I remember my parents proudly watching as I received my certificate at the graduation ceremony, and the image I had held in my mind since childhood, finally became a reality. At last, aged thirty five, I had achieved one of my life-long ambitions. Going back to university was one of the best decisions I had ever made, thanks to the amazing Fae guiding me all the way.

Fairy Godmother

Now, let me answer your burning question; who is this enigmatic Fae? Well, when I was about to get married, it was her voice that shouted at me to run. Over the years, I've learned how to hear her and she has guided me through every heartbreak, difficult situation and tough decision. Today, I have her to thank for all the 'right' choices I've made. With her help, resources, people and magical, synchronistic occurrences have often come my way, making my life so much easier, peaceful and successful. And yes, you too have a Fairy Godmother!

This is your amazing genie in a bottle, which has been tightly locked away in the basement of your castle, your subconscious mind, since you were a little child. Let's call this your *internal guidance system* (IGS), which is an in-built 'supernatural' power and one that we *all* have access to. You might think of it as your intuition, a quiet inner voice, gut feeling or, depending on your beliefs, a higher power. I must also point out that this is not at all a religious, but more of a psychological experience. However, it really does not matter how you choose to see it because it is always there, no matter your background or belief system. The trick is in learning the art of how to tune in so you can hear this inner voice.

As I love fairy tales, I like to think of mine as a 'Fairy Godmother'. Others like to think of it as their soul, higher self, guardian angel, spirit guide, mental counsellor or inner coach. I suggest that you give it a name that makes sense to you and which you are most comfortable with. For example, you could call it your genie, personal life navigator, sixth sense, instinctive knowing, intuitive awareness, internal voice or even a favourite superhero.

However, I suggest not calling it God because it is generally believed that such an omnipotent or Supreme Being is unlikely to talk with us mere mortals about our mundane, everyday matters. Although, as I already mentioned, it really does not matter what label you choose to give it as long as you understand that this extraordinary ability can help you in every aspect of your life.[9] For the purpose of this book, I will refer to your Fairy Godmother as 'IGS' and to mine as 'Fae'.

Once you understand the principles of how this 'resource' works and learn how to use it, your life will become very much easier, in more ways than you might imagine. I have taught many people about their inner guidance systems and used it myself to deal with countless problems; from solving difficult dilemmas and finding lost belongings to dealing with trouble at work, making important decisions about relationships, moving house and changing jobs.

For instance, during that same year, whilst applying to university, completing my NVQ and doing my job, I also took on board the arduous process of buying my first property. Sometimes, I still wonder how I managed to juggle it all. Taking such big life-changing steps pushed me far outside of my comfort zone. At every stage, I had to wade my way through unchartered bureaucratic waters and complex legal regulations.

At the time, I did not have a wise parent, friend or mentor to lean on. However, my good friend, Fae, was always there, standing beside me. She helped me at every point, from finding the right financial advisor, lending company and solicitor to selecting the best mortgage and the right university to suit my needs. She guided me in knowing which colleague to confide in and what to write on my applications. Thanks to Fae, I found the perfect little house, knew how much to offer and got an amazing deal.

At that time, I hardly had any money saved and I also needed to pay back my credit card debt in order to get a mortgage. My parents had given me just enough for a small deposit on the house but I had to find ways to manage the rest of my finances. Again, guided by Fae, I learned how to save money, curb my spending and create an income whilst studying.

I am certain that I would never have successfully managed the maze of paperwork, arranging finances, moving in and furnishing my new home, if it were not for the help of my brilliant Fae. I also would not have found suitable housemates, secured my place at university and quit my job, all in the space of a few months, without her guidance. At the same time, my relationship with Dan was rather turbulent and Fae's support, kind words and advice were invaluable. By the end of October 1998, I felt as though I had raced a marathon and come to a skidding halt, just in time to start my next trek up the mountain of studying at university again.

It is time now for me to give you the key to unlock the bottle and wake your genie. Your IGS can become your best friend and help you with everything from small day-to-day tasks to making those big, life-changing decisions. Once you have honed the skill of how to connect, it will not only guide you in the right direction but also provide you with an important tool for manifesting what you really want in life. This magical tool will support you through making relationship choices, from the initial stage of meeting someone, deciding if he/she is right for you to handling all those little, niggling everyday issues when living together.

Summon the Genie

Now, you may be wondering if *you* actually have an IGS at all. Let me assure you, every single human being on this planet has one and so do you. We were all born with it. As little children, it was normal for us to talk with our IGS or 'invisible friend' because we had a natural ability to connect and communicate with it. However, as we become adults, most of us forget that we once had this ability. The skill becomes dormant and remains buried in the depths of our subconscious minds.

In case you doubt whether you have one and if it will work for you, here are a few examples to illustrate how often it shows up in our everyday lives:

- As you are leaving the house, in the back of your mind, you get a tiny *knowing sense* that you forgot something. Then, on the way to your destination, it pops into your conscious mind and you remember the thing you forgot.
- You are at a party or out somewhere and offered something to eat. As your fingers reach out to take it, you get a feeling, perhaps in your belly that says, "No, don't eat it." Later, you realise that food didn't agree with you, and you get a stomach ache.

- You meet someone for the first time and from the start, you have a sense that something is *not quite right* about that person. However, you have no logical reason to dislike him/her and you dismiss the thought. At first, everything about her/him seems okay, normal and healthy, and there is no evidence to the contrary. Then, as time goes by, you get to know the person better and you discover that your initial instinct was correct.
- You are driving around a place you don't know very well, following your 'Sat Nav', and you start to have a strange feeling that you are going the wrong way. You ignore the feeling and continue to follow the digital guidance system. Eventually, you find it has taken you to a different location and your hunch was right after all.

I am sure you can think of many other such occurrences of when your inner voice has tried to speak with you. Your IGS shows itself through that quiet, knowing sense, the whisper in your head or a gut feeling you occasionally have.

Unfortunately, most people tend to ignore it, so this resource remains suppressed and untrained. As with any other human faculty, if we don't use it, we lose it. However, when you learn to use and sharpen this sixth sense, you will instantly recognise it working and be able to use it for much greater purposes than just finding your lost keys.

So, how does this actually work? According to science, this ability allows you to tap into your deeper subconscious mind and communicate with it; your hidden intelligence. Our brains produce different wavelengths of mild electrical energy which vary, depending on whether we are awake, half-asleep or in deep sleep. It is the state you are in just before you fall asleep or when you are very relaxed or daydreaming, which I want to bring your attention to, as this is the magic zone. This is the frequency level in your brain known as the 'Alpha' wavelength which is between 7-12 Hz/sec.[10] At this level, we are naturally dipping into our subconscious and creative minds. This is where we can connect to our IGS, Fairy Godmother or intuitive self.

Your subconscious brain is also where all of your life's experiences are stored: your childhood, past history and all memories as well as where your everyday needs, habits and preferences are recorded, such as your 'default programmes' or routine behaviours.[11] This is the part of you that is in tune with your deepest desires, goals and dreams. Tapping into your IGS can help you decipher exactly how you should move forward towards your best possible future and attract the right person into your life. But only, if you learn how to hear it.

So, how do we access this incredible resource? Well, there is a magic castle in the sky where your Fairy Godmother lives and you will need to sit in a lotus position, in your cave and go into a deep trance for forty days and nights. Then, you must learn to transcend your body and become one with the eternal...

No, no, no! I'm only joking! It requires nothing that difficult. All you need to do is allow your brain to calm down and get yourself into a nice, relaxed, comfortable state so that you can enter that magical place in your mind. This is how you access your subconscious brain and it can be done simply by going into a gentle level of meditation.

You may be surprised to know that your brain actually enters this level several times a day. For instance, when you awake in the morning and remain with your eyes closed in bed, your brain is at the Alpha level. Usually, you experience a half-asleep, dreamlike state and your mind may replay parts of dreams that you had but at the same time, you may also have clear, lucid and creative thoughts. During the day, your brain is also at this level if you find yourself drifting off in your mind whilst doing something repetitive or mundane, such as driving to work or sitting watching a boring programme.

When you learn to meditate, you enter this level of the mind in a more controlled and conscious way. Whilst in this relaxed state of mind, you will be able to access deeper thought processes, default programmes and beliefs and change them. Or you can find solutions to problems, gain insights and have creative ideas.

Your IGS may be rather elusive but I will show you how to pin it down. First of all, there are a few important elements you need to bear in mind in order to summon your IGS. Just like the genie in the bottle, you have to learn how to rub the lamp in the right way and know exactly which magic words to use for making wishes and consciously communicating with it.

- **Belief**: If you are very sceptical about this method and think it cannot work, then you will get exactly what you believe. On the other hand, if you can accept that there might be a dormant ability inside your subconscious brain and allow yourself to entertain this possibility, it is more likely to work for you. Once you have used it a few times on small things, your belief will grow. The more you practice and believe in the process, the more automatically it will work for you.

- **Trust**: If you worry a lot and question your own ability, it probably won't work as well. Of course, it is natural to worry and you should not expect that perfection straight away, so give yourself time to slowly build your confidence. As you grow in your ability, you will gain more faith in yourself and learn to trust the process. Just tell yourself, "I *can* do this," and "I am learning".

- **Practise and patience**: The only way to gain more trust and belief in getting the IGS to work is through regular practise. Just like learning to ride a bike or cook a meal, you can expect that, at first, you may wobble and fall off the bike or be confused about the ingredients. You must prepare well, practise the new skill often, remember what you've learned and most importantly, have patience. Eventually, it will be so natural that you won't need to try and it will just become a habit. You will know exactly when and how your IGS speaks to you and be able to turn to it at anytime.

You are now ready to take the first exciting step to meet your personal IGS and start creating magic in your life! The following exercise is a visualising meditation, which I am sure you will enjoy. It will take you deeper than the ones we did before and you will use more creative thinking. The trick is not to concentrate or try too hard or *make yourself* see something. It is better to relax, trust your imagination and just let things flow. If you find your mind wandering off in a totally different direction, just become aware of it and gently steer it back to the instructions.

LESSON 5: Your Inner Guidance System

A. Meeting Your Fairy Godmother

Before you begin, think of a question or a little problem that has recently been on your mind. It is best to select a small issue that is of no great consequence and the outcome will not matter too much.

Start by simply reading the following instructions aloud into a voice recording device or app. Then, relax and listen to the recording with your earphones. It is better to do the exercise this way rather than try to remember all the instructions with your eyes closed as that will keep you from being able to fully relax.

During the exercise, allow your imagination to run free and just let your mind be spontaneous and creative. Try not to be too correct, logical or question whatever comes up.

As before, choose a time and place when you can be alone and undisturbed.

1. Sit down in a comfortable position with your arms beside you, your legs uncrossed and your feet on the floor. If you are lying down, lie on your back and place your hands and legs in the most relaxed position for you.
2. Take three nice, long, deep breaths and with each breath, feel your body becoming more relaxed.
3. As you breathe in, allow a feeling of calm and centeredness to come into your body and mind. As you breathe out, release any tension or worries.
4. Tell yourself you are now deeply relaxed and that when you come out of this meditation, you will feel completely awake and refreshed.

5. Slowly count backwards from 10 to 1 in your head. With each number, focus on relaxing a different part of your body. Start with your feet and work your way up to the top of your head. Feel the muscles relax, especially around your neck, shoulders, face, eyes and jaw.

6. Now, imagine you are alone and walking along the beach or outside in a beautiful, natural place that you love to be in. The scenery is calm and relaxing, and the weather is just right. This is your very own place of peace and relaxation.

7. Look around and take in the view with all your senses. Notice the sounds, the smells and feel the air on your face. Spend a few moments enjoying this scenery and tell yourself, "It feels so good to be here".

8. As you continue to walk, you see a figure in the distance walking slowly towards you. This can be a real or an imaginary person. As she/he comes closer, you see, feel or perceive the way he/she looks and his/her demeanour. Allow your imagination to create whatever comes to mind. You may feel like you are just making it up.

9. Know that this person is your IGS and cares deeply for you. She or he is very wise, knowledgeable and always knows the right answer and how to help you.

10. Your IGS now approaches you, greets you warmly and tells you his/her name. You have the feeling of already knowing each other for a long, long time. You feel very comfortable in each other's company and walk along the path together.

11. After a while, you see a walled garden with a tall gate ahead of you. You both enter through the gate to find yourselves in a beautiful garden. Take a look around and enjoy the tranquillity. Then, walk along the path leading to a house and go inside.

12. You now go through a door and find yourselves standing inside a very special room. It is furnished perfectly to your taste and you

feel very much at home here. Take it all in and enjoy being in this space. To one side, there is a comfy sofa and in front of it a big TV-like screen on the wall. On another side of the room is a large table with a computer, gadgets, tools and containers on it. This is your own wonderful space, filled with all the things that you might need to find answers, solve problems and do magical transformative work.

13. You and your IGS sit down on the sofa, facing the screen. Beside you, there is a remote control to operate the screen.

14. Now, speak with your IGS and explain the question or problem you have in mind. Imagine he/she is answering you. Allow any spontaneous thoughts, words or feelings to arise and do not force an answer.

15. As you become more practised in doing this, you can imagine switching on the TV screen or using the computer or any other item available in the room to help you. Simply ask your IGS and let him/her do the work to find the answers for you.

16. Enjoy this time with your IGS and spend as long as you want in your special room.

17. When you are ready, tell your IGS how much you appreciate her/his help and say goodbye. Your IGS stays in the room and you come out of the house, through the garden and back out of the gate.

18. You have now returned to your peaceful place in nature. Walk back down the path along which you first came.

19. Take a deep breath and let go of all that you have seen and experienced.

20. Slowly count back from 1 to 10 whilst allowing your senses to become more aware of your physical body.

21. Tell yourself you will feel fine and awake when you open your eyes. Take your time to return to the present and open your eyes when you are ready. Have a good stretch and feel glad for having had a good relaxing meditation.

22. Lastly, in your notebook, write down a short description of your IGS and any thoughts, feelings you perceived whilst talking with her/him as well as any answers regarding your question or problem. Include today's date. Do not try to analyse or make sense of anything at this stage.

The first time you take this journey into your imaginary world, you may think you are making it all up. It may feel awkward or silly, and seem like child's play. Don't worry! That is exactly what it is supposed to feel like. Initially, just consider it to be practice runs and allow your mind to spontaneously conjure up anything it wants. Simply allow yourself to get used to relaxing and letting your creative thoughts flow.

As you are doing the meditation, you will probably find your logical brain kicking in and trying to make sense of things or telling you how it *should* be. This is quite normal when you first start using your imagination in this way. Just be patient with yourself and accept that you have not used this part of your brain much since you were a little child. Naturally, it is likely to be a little rusty.

After doing this exercise a few times, you can omit step 8-10 about your first encounter with your IGS and simply meet her or him in your special room. When you become more practised with this meditation, you can do other interesting and clever things, such as looking into the future or seeing an outcome for a project or something you want to manifest. Simply ask your IGS to show you a video on the screen and imagine watching the event or scenario taking place at that future time. If you have a relationship issue or something complicated going on in your life, you can ask your IGS to help you understand and sort out the problem.

Sometimes, the answers you get are not at all as you might have expected or are ready to hear. In that case, just write it all down and try not to dwell on it. Then, when you do the meditation again, ask your IGS to help you understand the previous answers and give you some further clarification.

B. Learning to Hear the Whispers

At first, most people often find it difficult to 'hear' the answers they get from their IGS. This is because we, as humans, are used to talking and communicating verbally. We usually expect to hear the voice in words or sounds in response from the other person we are talking with. However, in the subconscious world, this is not how things are communicated. Here are some points to help you understand how to *hear* the answers from your IGS.

1. When you first begin doing the meditation and talking with your IGS, it is better to avoid asking difficult questions regarding issues you are very worried about. For instance, "Is he still in love with me?" Then, what will likely happen is that your very clever subconscious brain/IGS might give you either a direct hit, which you may not be ready to hear, and you'll dismiss it or it will avoid answering the question. Meanwhile, your conscious brain will step in and give you a gentler, kinder answer which you would rather hear but it won't be the actual truth.

2. If your thought processes tend to be visual, most likely, you will find it easier to imagine the scenarios mentioned in the meditation as pictures or videos in your mind. If, however, you are more inclined towards auditory thinking, you may find it difficult to 'see' images in your mind. Instead, your brain will imagine things in a different way, such as hearing sounds, music or strings of words. On the other hand, if you are more 'kinaesthetic', you might mentally experience having a physical feeling or tactile sensation or even perhaps,

a movement through an environment.12 Some people find they have a combination of all three sensory modes; seeing videos in full colour with sound and feeling textures. Or perhaps you may have a less vivid sensory imagination but simply have a knowing sense or inner awareness, which spontaneously appears in your conscious thoughts. Whatever your imagination brings forth, allow it to be and accept that this is how your mind works.

3. One of the most common concerns about this exercise is, 'How do I *know the difference* between hearing my own thoughts and the voice of my IGS?' It takes a while to distinguish between the two and quite often, people find there is little difference. The only way I know for certain is by the timing of the answer. You will know it is your IGS talking if it is an immediate response or it arrives when you are not expecting it. However, if you find yourself dwelling on the question, trying to figure it out, then it will be your problem solving, conscious brain at work and not your IGS answering you.

   During the meditation, you simply have to bring to mind the dilemma or issue. You will often find that as you are formulating the question, the answer will often pop up in your mind instantaneously – this is your IGS answering. Or you will get nothing straight away and have to wait a while. Usually, if you can present the question and forget about it consciously, your subconscious mind will take over and your IGS will deliver the answer unexpectedly, whilst you are distracted doing something else. The process is similar to when you are trying really hard to remember the name of an actor or artist, and no matter how much you wrack your brain, you just cannot retrieve the answer. Then, after you give up and go to the bathroom, you have a 'Eureka moment'.

4. Another way to hear the whispers from your IGS is when you become conscious of having specific reoccurring thoughts or ideas. Unexpectedly, one thought will keep popping up in your mind and it will happen when you are busy at work or doing something

completely unrelated. This might not necessarily be an answer to the question you presented to your IGS. However, it could be something that you need to pay attention to. You will probably find that you keep pushing it aside but this is your very caring IGS calling you to take action on something quite important.

For example, you may find yourself thinking about an ex, an old friend or relative for no apparent reason. Consciously, you really don't want to think about that person, and you have no inclination to contact him/her, but your IGS knows better and will try to tell you so. It could be that this is an early warning to help you avoid something bad. Or it might be that you are harbouring some hidden, negative feelings about your ex, which you now need to face in order to heal.

5. You could have a dream that gives you a metaphoric answer or you may see an object, image or scene on a film that grabs your attention. You might overhear something or notice several unrelated occurrences with a similar theme and correlate them in your mind. This happened to me when two different friends said the same thing without my asking, and neither had any contact with the other. At the same time, I found myself searching for answers about my future and life's direction. Thus, all the signs started pointing me in one direction – to go back to college.

6. Once you have presented your IGS with a question or concern, there are many other ways you may receive a message, answer or understanding. For instance, you could be outside taking a stroll, walking the dog or driving your car and your mind drifts into that daydream, Alpha brainwave state. You remember something from your long-forgotten past and enjoy a nostalgic moment. Suddenly, you realise that this memory is directly related to the question you had asked your IGS some days ago and the solution or answer becomes clear and makes perfect sense.

Once you have done this meditation a few times, you will become more familiar with your IGS and how he or she prefers to communicate with you. Whilst you are new to this method, it is best to simply notice your own thoughts and feelings, as and when they come up, and just note it all down. Initially, I suggest you don't act upon any answers you receive until you feel sure that it is right for you.

C. Asking Specific Questions

When you first start, it is best to use 'closed' questions which are easier to answer and require only a yes or no response. A closed question is one that usually begins with the words 'is/am/are, do/does, have/has, can, should or will'. When you become more accustomed to receiving replies, you can ask more 'open' questions, beginning with 'what, where, when, how, why or who', that require more detailed answers.

Do not ask several questions at one time. Keep your questions straightforward and brief. If your request is not worded clearly or specifically enough, your IGS can easily get confused and may not answer you.

As I mentioned, it is better to start with smaller issues and build up your confidence first. Leave the life-changing issues for later and when you have developed your intuition and tuning-in abilities more. When you become more adept at talking with your IGS and hearing answers, you will be able to ask more serious types of questions. Here are some examples of important questions that you could try once you are more practised. Notice how each question asks about only one specific issue.

- Am I still harbouring feelings for X deep down?
- Am I really ready to move on?

- Are my feelings being respected?
- Is it time to start looking again?
- Is Y being genuine?
- Do I need to go on holiday with Z?
- Does X still care about me?
- Has my heart healed enough?
- Have I learnt the lesson yet?
- Can I take the risk?
- Shall I offer to pay off the debt?
- Should I talk to Y about..?
- Should I stay in this job/house/relationship?
- Will Z ever spend more time with the kids?
- Will it get better if I wait?

The trick is in developing your ability to become more aware of your own thoughts, responses and intuitive feelings as they arise. At first, you may be forgiven for logging every thought or thinking that everything that occurs is a message from your IGS. You might find yourself imagining all the song lyrics you hear as meaningful messages or every emotion you feel as being a 'sign'. Don't worry – tuning in takes practise and you will eventually learn to differentiate between what is and isn't significant. It is important to allow yourself time to make mistakes and hone the skill slowly. Keep notes in your notebook of when you do receive genuine, positive 'hits', no matter how small they might be, as this will build your confidence.

For me, the best time to talk with my Fae is either just before sleep or early in the morning, when I first awake. I tend to ask a question or pose a problem the night before and in the morning, as soon as I bring the issue to mind, the answer arrives. Sometimes, it appears a little later, whilst doing my morning routine, or perhaps much later in the day, when I'm not focused on it at all. My mind is very visual, and I usually see images on my mental screen or pictures just floating around in my thoughts that indicate the answer. More often, I will have a knowing feeling or hear my own voice answering the questions during my meditations.

When I first started doing this kind of meditation, I wouldn't get any answers at all from Fae. I would only feel her friendly presence near me in my special room. But as I became more experienced, I began to understand that her way of telling me things was through that quiet sense of knowingness. Whenever I was trying too hard or feeling stressed, I wouldn't hear her at all. Today, I am so adept at speaking with her that I hardly need to try to go into a meditation level but can simply close my eyes and think.

This ability is more than just following your intuition or gut feeling. It is an enhanced ability to tune in to your inner wisdom and insightful sixth sense. Having done the exercises and switched on your inner guidance system, your life will now never be the same again. You will automatically find yourself, not just reacting to situations, but asking important questions first, and gaining greater understanding about your lessons and deciding on appropriate actions or difficult dilemmas.

When you are more accustomed to the process, you will naturally become more aware of your everyday needs, wants and desires. This, in turn, aligns you with your life's purpose and direction. Thus, as you make more authentic day-to-day choices based on *your* needs, so too, will your life become more fulfilling and attuned to your heart's true desire.

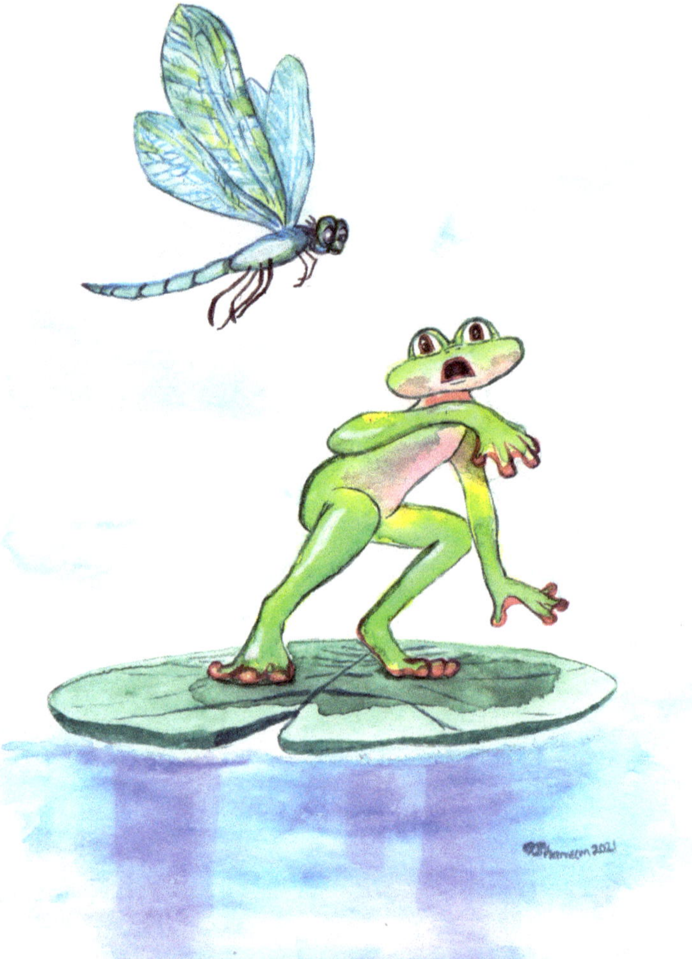

7. The Dragon's Lair

"Why ever do I listen to that owl?" she muttered as she cautiously entered the dark cavern. This was not her idea of adventure. "Dragons, indeed! There's no such thing. I'll show her there's nothing down here."

Suddenly, there was a rumbling and bustling and a great gust of foul smoky air blew passed her. The princess froze, her eyes wide, heart thumping. She put one hand over her nose and the other held out her wand. "Who goes there?" she called out bravely.
No one answered.

She took a few steps forward but could see nothing. Trembling, she lit a match holding it up to the dark. As her eyes grew accustomed to the gloom, just there, a few paces ahead, sat an ugly looking dragon! It blinked and grinned at her with a mouthful of food. The floor was strewn with fish bones, rotting pumpkins and other rubbish.

"Well, if I'd known I'd have company, I might have saved you some," said the dragon in a deep, gruff voice.
She peered a little closer. "Why, you are not at all fearsome," said the princess, putting away her wand.

Another Frog

The DJ was playing some upbeat tunes and preparing his playlists for the rest of the night. The night club was a smart, swanky place, right in the centre of the main nightlife part of town. It was furnished with plush seats, neon lights, mirrors and glass. The bar staff, in their dark polo shirts, were courteous as I ordered my usual. Taking my drink, I wandered over to one of the tall, narrow tables and settled myself on a stool.

Nodding to the rhythm, I pulled out my mobile phone from my small evening bag and pressed some buttons, trying to look busy. The last time I had been here, it was with a friend but this evening, I had bravely come alone. It was still early with only a scattering of people around and more were bound to come later. I was feeling happy, confident and hopeful that there would be a nice crowd and a chance for a good dance.

This was a fresh start for me, a new chapter in my life. Living near the sea had been a lifelong dream, and now, I could proudly say that I had made it come true. Having moved into my new house, in this easy-going, coastal town and starting a new job as a training instructor, I felt thoroughly pleased with myself. The only thing missing was that, apart from my work colleagues, I hardly knew anyone else here and so, it was time to build a new social life.

It had been almost five years since Bob and I were together and at 38, the clock was ticking… loudly! Yes, five laborious years of trying to date but meeting no one. Well, none that I felt could qualify for a decent relationship. I was so tired of heart-breaking holiday encounters and the hopeless online dating 'matches'. Now, I needed to find someone who was closer to home. And I was not going to meet anyone sitting at home, watching TV.

It was a Friday evening so I put on a pretty outfit, my heels and makeup, and then drove to the local nightspot. As usual, on such nights, I would start out feeling hopeful, calm and playing it cool. "Come on, girl – you can do this," I reassured myself after sitting there for almost an hour. "You've travelled the world, handled crazy situations and met hundreds of weird and wonderful people from every corner. Sitting alone in a nightclub at the back end of Essex isn't exactly a stretch."

As I leisurely lit up another slim, dark cigarette, I remembered how much easier it had been in Florida and South America. There, I could go to any bar, in any town, and feel perfectly comfortable. The atmosphere was different and I could sit alone easily, as a woman without anyone batting an eyelid. The people were always more friendly, and usually, before I'd even finished ordering my coffee or drink, there would be someone happily making conversation with me. Here, however, the culture was quite different and I felt rather out of place, as though people were raising a condescending eyebrow at me.

Eventually, the place started to fill up, and three guys arrived, got their drinks and parked themselves at the other end of my table. I checked my watch and then my phone as though I were waiting for someone. "A lady never makes the first move," I reminded myself and continued to look preoccupied. It took a while, but finally, after a few confidence-building beers, one of the guys leaned over and started talking with me. He had no idea just how relieved and grateful I was for his company.

"Yer not from 'round 'ere, are ya?" he queried in a thick accent.
"No," I answered. My princess charm dial was turned all the way up as I played my 'give nothing away but a smile' card. It was not him who had caught my eye but one of his friends, the tall, dark-haired one with the distinctly South African accent.

It wasn't until much later, when the other two had clearly given up trying to impress me that he eventually spoke. He apologised for the drunkenness of his friends and I smiled, saying it was no bother. Then, I continued to have a refreshingly intelligent conversation with this green-eyed stranger. It turned out that he too, had also travelled a lot and had many stories to tell.

The first few dates with Al were great and I enjoyed his dry wit and sharp opinions. He turned out to be a gentleman with a kind heart underneath his rugged exterior. It was delightful to meet someone who lived nearby and not miles away, someone with whom I could discuss common interests about people, politics and the places we'd visited. As usual, it was always during the first exciting wave of being in a new relationship that my wistful heart would bring the fairy tale back to life, entertaining notions of a happy-ever-after together. But, just as quickly, I would wrestle those ideas back into the 'Not now, far too soon!' box and hide them away in the cupboard of my dreams.

After a while, Al's true nature began to surface and I witnessed his anger and frustration come pouring out towards his ex for having taken away the one thing he held most precious, his beloved little daughter. Following a rather horrid divorce, he was obviously still recovering from a broken heart and hauling a barge-full of hurt around. He would not stop talking about his broken family but, as always, I listened sympathetically and began to suspect that secretly, he was still in love with his ex-girlfriend.

By amusing coincidence, and as the gods would have it, his ex worked at the same training centre as I did. Interestingly, she seemed to be a white, South African version of myself with a similar build, looks, character and temperament. How funny, I thought. Of course, as you know, we all tend to attract the same 'types'. I never found out if she knew about Al and I, but I made sure that our paths didn't cross too often.

The relationship continued for a few months. Then, one Sunday morning, having lain awake most of the night, I decided to leave his place early and tiptoed out into the cool fresh air at five thirty in the morning. It had been yet another long night of tedious, one-sided conversations about his ex and how much better his old life was back in South Africa. I drove the scenic route home, along the coast and enjoyed the calm of daybreak, thinking that, yet again, here I was in another relationship, doing all the giving.

When I had arrived the night before, the fridge had been empty. He had not made anything to eat, although he used to enjoy cooking for us both when we had first met. So, we ordered pizza, which arrived very late, and it seemed that it wasn't the only thing that had lost its warmth. During the whole evening, I couldn't recall if he asked a single question about my day, my week, or anything about how I was. Recently, he had become even more detached and unaffectionate, emotionally and physically, towards me.

I parked along the embankment and took a short walk along the promenade, breathing in the salty sea air and pondering my next step. "I know what I have do," I thought, "but why does it have to always end like this? Why, why, oh why do I always have this same old thing happening?!" Glaring at the sky, I pleaded with God, "Really? What did I do so wrong this time?! What is it I am not getting? Please, tell me!" I was utterly fed up and disappointed. "Fae, why didn't you warn me?"

Strangely, I had very few tears to shed this time. It was as though my heart had already decided it was done with him and just wanted to move on. As I had been the only one calling and arranging our dates recently, I decided to see what would happen if I didn't call or do anything for a while. Eventually, he did call me about three weeks later and made various excuses. We talked for a while and then, quite amicably, both decided that it was over. There was no need to make a fuss over something that had never really taken off the ground. For once, I didn't feel as heartbroken as before, perhaps because no hearts were actually invested, to begin with. All that was left was the same old lingering feeling of sadness and loneliness that prevailed.

Facing the Truth

Until then, it seemed obvious to the princess that all she needed was just to find her prince, and then, they would live happily ever after. After all, this frogling had grown up to be a fine, fairly well-balanced woman with a clear head, big heart and no major issues. She had a good career with a stable income and was also a proud home-owner. The few friends she had were loyal, caring and dependable. She had matured enough, learned about self-worth and accepted herself as she was. What more would such a princess have to do to qualify for being a worthy life-partner?

*Alas, for most of her adult years, the princess had only attracted frogs and toads, none of which were eligible to be her forever prince. She didn't understand why, or rather didn't want to know why, until one day she opened her heart to the truth. You see, it is a well-known fact, that when it comes to relationships, 'like attracts like'. She would now learn that if she wished to be with a prince, then **she** must first **think** like a princess.*

To my amazement, over the following months, I was taken on an eye-opening journey that profoundly shifted my inner world. Since that morning when I had ranted at the gods, it was as though Fae had taken charge and decided it was time for stronger measures. Now, I was about to wake up to the actual truth which I had never acknowledged before, and that had lain deeply buried in the basement of my psyche. I was going to learn a vital lesson and one that I certainly had not asked for, at least not consciously.

Deep down, I always felt there was something missing and had assumed it was just the unending longing to love and be loved. However, one thing I knew for sure was that every time a relationship came to an end, there was always a lesson to be learnt. So, as usual, after yet another heart break, I went to my special room every night before sleep and asked Fae, about what I needed to learn. I tried to keep an open mind even though my conscious brain was saying, "What else could I possibly need to learn? Hadn't I been given enough lessons?"

Then, it happened! The reality I had been avoiding started to unveil itself. For so many years, I had been trying to figure out exactly what was going wrong in my relationships and either blaming myself for things going wrong or thinking, as several well-meaning friends and family had pointed out, that I was too picky. Until then, Fae had never given me any straight answers to this perplexing question but now, instead of her usual smiling presence and vagueness, she began to give me much clearer understandings. Slowly and gently, almost as though a kind, wise aunt was leading me by the hand, she guided me through finding and opening the heavy baggage that I had unknowingly carried for decades.

"Come, look," she said and indicated the screen in front of us. It was a scene that had taken place years ago, which I had completely forgotten about. My housemate, Kay, and I were sitting on my bed looking through my box of old photos. We were chatting as I reminisced about my younger years, showing her photos of my family, travels and old friends from the ships. After a while, Kay started to pull out one photo here and another one there from the various packs and put them to one side, face down.

"What *are* you doing?" I asked. "I had them all in order. You'll get them mixed up," I said, with mock annoyance.

"Nothing," she said, grinning, "You just carry on". So, we continued until we'd gone through all the packets of photos.

When we were done, she eventually took the photos she had selected and laid them face up in front of me, saying, "Look – what do you notice?"

I stared at the photos. "You've selected all my previous boyfriends. And?" I replied, a little defensively.

"Oh, you don't see anything? Look closer! What do you notice about all of them?" she insisted, tapping a finger at their faces.

I inspected each photo, taking a closer look. "No idea," I said, confused. Kay started giggling and made a silly face at me. "They are all the same! Haa ha ha!!" she exclaimed and fell into rolls of laughter.

"Huh? What do you mean? No, they are not!" I argued, failing to see her humour. "That one was years ago at college. And that one was Ted, the one I married. And this one, I met him at my workplace. And well, this one is Dan, as you already know – "

"No, no, no," she interrupted. "It's not about where they're from or how you met them." She picked out two and held them in front of my eyes. "Look at their faces. They all *look* the same!" Kay was thoroughly amused. Then, handing me back the photos, she left my room, still giggling.

Later on, I took another careful look through the photos before putting them away and realised that she was right. They did, indeed, look similar.

"So?" I turned back to Fae after watching the scene. "Yes, well, I guess I have a 'type' it seems. I know I always go for the same tall, dark-haired, dark-eyed types. Rather stereotypical, I guess. So, what's the problem?" I was not keen on this topic of conversation.

She smiled and I understood her thoughts immediately, "You must recognise that you always attract the same *type* of person. It is not just in the way they look – it is the way they *are*. You have a pattern."

This was a revelation! I had always believed that I was progressing in my relationships by learning the lessons and being more cautious each time. I pondered this for a while and began to realise that there actually was a pattern in the type of person I kept attracting.

"Other than the superficial physical looks, what else did they have in common?" I asked Fae. And so, we continued to analyse my past, watching more scenes and discussing them together.

Over the coming months, I was shown more scenes such as one from some years ago at university, about a conversation with my good friend, Steph. Again, it was a conversation that I had forgotten about. We were in the study room where I was lamenting over my recent break-up with Dan and feeling rather sorry for myself. I knew that Steph would lend a kindly ear.

"Come on – you'll be okay and find another nice guy," she consoled, "you always do."
I looked at her with feigned indignity. "What do you mean: I *always* do? I don't just want another guy. I want to find the *one*, someone who wants me for me. The real me. I am tired of guys who are just interested in me for what I look like or because I am a laugh. It has to be someone who really *gets* me."

Steph hesitated, then looked at me squarely and said, "Well, you're a psychologist and want to be a coach, don't you? What would a coach say to someone who keeps attracting the same kind of guy?" Then, she added with a little more sympathy, "I think you know the answer. It's time, my lovely, to take your own medicine".

I did not want to face the answer to Steph's question back then, but now, as I thought again about the question, I said to Fae, "Well, I suppose I'd ask my client, what did all his or her previous partners have in common? Yes, yes, of course, I know all that stuff about repeating patterns. But my relationships, well they were all very different. Maybe early on, it was about the lack of money. But now, in general, they have very little in common. There are no common denominators between any of them. Well, apart from being with me, that is," I said, grinning. And after a moment, it clicked, "OH!" I gasped.

I stopped, mouth open and stared at the screen. A light bulb had flashed on in my head. "Oh, my goodness! That's it, isn't it? Of course! The answer is right there – it's so simple." *I* was the thing they all had in common! *I* was the common denominator. It was a hard truth to face.

As we watched this scene, Fae shared her thoughts with me but without Steph's gentleness. "So, if you're always attracting the same type, shouldn't you be asking what *you* are doing to attract those men? What kind of energy are you sending out?"

I had heard about the 'Law of Attraction' but hadn't given much thought as to how it affected my love life. "Quite often you have gone out with the underlying intention that you must find someone and are always looking and wanting a man. If you exude that sort of feeling, then guess what you will attract? Whatever your energy is transmitting at the very beginning, when you first meet someone, that is exactly the kind of energy you will attract into your relationship," said Fae. She paused giving me time to think.

"Do you remember what you were feeling and thinking that night in the bar when you first met Al? Were you being your true, genuine self, the person you normally are when you're relaxed and with friends? Or were you acting and behaving in a different way, like something other than you actually are?" Now, it was all beginning to make sense. My energy that night was probably somewhat overconfident, coquettish even and perhaps a little arrogant. It was one that gave off an air of 'I can attract any man I want using my feminine wiles' and I was most definitely on the 'hunt' to meet someone.

Since the frog had become a princess, she was quite aware of this 'charm' which she would use to her advantage. She would always hope that once she had made her catch, her mask could come off, and then, her hero would gradually get to know her true self and appreciate her deeper qualities. Hence, it was not surprising that she had always attracted men who only took her at face value. It was the cold, stark truth and although, tough to admit, she was beginning to realise that she had always faked being a princess.

Next, and more unsettling, came the revelations of how I had acquired these patterns in the first place. My psychologist's mind needed to get to the root of the behaviour, so that I could understand the reason and learn the lesson fully. Again, Fae took me through several experiences from my early childhood with my parents. These were cold, harsh truths, which I had never wanted to face, but they were essential to my inner growth and healing.

Fae guided me through watching various scenes on the screen of the way my mother and father had behaved with each other when I was very young. Being able to simply 'observe' and watch these scenes as a witness rather than being part of it, made it a little easier and less emotional. My parents would often argue, each voicing their differences loudly. Then, they would turn cold and for days there was silence between them. Usually, their arguments stemmed from a lack of money but I am sure there were other deeper, unspoken issues. The atmosphere at home seemed to have little balance and there was never any long-term peace in their relationship. To my young mind, it always felt uneasy and turbulent. Now, it was becoming clear how the roller coaster ride with Ted was a recreation of my parent's relationship.

My father often seemed aloof, absorbing himself in his work. He was naturally a quiet, reserved man and tried to avoid confrontations. Shutting off from my mother was his way of coping and it was the only way he could handle her excessive emotionality. Her usual complaint was that my father didn't *do enough* to make money. In her eyes, he was never good enough and she was very critical of everything that he actually did. As an adult, I became aware that this was *her* distorted view but I was unaware of just how much these untruths had taken a hold in my unconscious beliefs about men during those highly impressionable formative years. Until then, I had no idea that I had absorbed such negative beliefs about men and how that had affected my behaviour towards men.

The Buried Past

Over the coming years, on my healing journey, I was shown many more 'films', revisiting my past and remembering stories I had forgotten. Some were very surprising, as they had happened long before the age of five which is when most of us start having a conscious memory of experiences. Each time I came out of my meditations, I was in awe of the astonishing capacity of our brains that are able to store every tiny detail in our lives, from the day we are born. I felt humbled, enlightened and very grateful that I could now use this remarkable tool in so many ways. It had also become the best therapist I could have ever asked for.

Here are some of the insights I uncovered:

- As a young adult, the kind of men I tended to attract were rather self-centred, irresponsible and/or overly dependent on me because my default programme was to please. By being the one who gave and gave, I attracted those whose default programmes were only to take and take. Therefore, I needed to learn how to receive, too.
- When my heart was filled with *neediness* and a constant hunger for love, I attracted someone who was equally desperate and needy. He too, consciously or unconsciously, believed that there was a 'lack' in his life. The more desperate I felt, the more desperation I attracted.
- If ever I found myself in a rebound relationship, I only attracted the same kind of energy I was generating at that time. That 'reactionary' behaviour was a crutch to make me feel better about myself but which was only ever a temporary fix.
- My mother had pushed me into having that marriage ceremony because she loved me and believed it was the only route to keep me safe and secure.
- My father's so-called inadequacies were untrue and entirely imagined by my mother. They stemmed from her own sense of inadequacy, fears and childhood experiences. In reality, my father was a highly admired man. He was successful in his chosen field and well supported by all of his extended family, friends and colleagues throughout his life.
- Growing up, I had learned that having loving relationships meant pain, anguish and turmoil. We never saw much in the way of love, joy or empathy between my parents and any 'making up' was done behind closed doors. This toxic programme was deeply ingrained and needed to be pulled out from the root.

- I used to believe that affection, kindness, and gentleness were never given freely. It had to be earned by giving gifts and working very hard, which was another false programme that needed overhauling.
- It was ridiculous of me to expect Ted to make me a priority and love me more than he did when *I* had no idea how to give myself priority or love myself. This has been one of my greatest lessons and I am still working on it.

As time went on, many difficult truths were revealed. Some were hard to swallow and gave me headaches and sleepless nights. Slowly, as the stories unfolded, I began to make sense of my unconscious behaviours and the choices I'd made over the years; the reasons behind why I had fallen for particular men.

I learned of the 'programmes' instilled in childhood and the motivations behind my false pride. Those ingrained beliefs had steered my thoughts, expectations and behaviours, in not only my romantic, but also in some of my work, friends and family relationships. These were the nasty but essential truths which I had to face in order to better understand my deeper self.

Several years later, whilst I was on my grieving journey, Fae took me on another round of unveiling more hidden truths from my past. By then, I had grown in self-awareness and was more willing to accept these revelations. Thus, I learned even greater lessons:

- In the past, most of the men I had been involved with were unavailable, either emotionally, physically or geographically. Their half-hearted interest underlined my own belief in the 'lack of love' that was missing in my life. It taught me that pouring out too much love on those who don't deserve me was a sign of my own insecurity and desperation to be loved. I needed to learn I was worthwhile, valuable and loveable just as I am.

- I was finally able to be brutally honest with myself and admit that I never actually wanted to be a mother. Looking back, I was not a 'goo-goo, gaa-gaa' kind of girl and would never feel the urge to hold a baby whenever I saw one. It was hard to accept but the *need* to have a baby which so many of my female peers felt was not as compelling for me. It simply was not a part of my hard wiring. The desire I *thought* I had was entirely driven by social conditioning and the need to please. So, with relief, I let all that go.

- At various times in my life, I had been the subject of manipulation, backstabbing and downright malicious behaviour, not in my relationships, but by bosses, certain friends and family members. Again, another lesson about self-worth. I needed to learn how to stand up for myself and not let bullies win.

- In my latter years, I had attracted men with mild psychological issues, such as Autism, ADHD, personality disorders and emotional dysfunction. As my career started to take a psychological route, my desire was to attract people who needed my help but I needed to learn how to keep it to clients only. I had to be more wary of what I wished for and set clearer boundaries for my personal relationships.

- Their psychological problems also highlighted the fact that I had to face my own issues which stemmed from childhood. The dysfunction and insecurity I experienced in my own family gave rise to my greatest fears, that of being inadequate, unlovable and unwanted. This, of course, manifested in my adult relationships as being misunderstood, uncared for and unappreciated. I now had to learn how to face and conquer those fears.

Meeting My Dragon

Opening my mind to learning gave me a greater perspective and an objective understanding of the reasons why I had attracted and pursued those previous relationships. Now, I needed to find out what to do with this knowledge and how to change things. If I stopped being the over-confident, fake princess, would I become a cowering wall flower again? How and what other aspects of myself could I show instead to attract the right kind of man? How could I be more genuine and authentic when meeting someone new?

It was time to stop those old patterns and start adopting new ones. The first essential step was to accept that beneath every habitual behaviour, or 'default program', lay a *need* or motivation. This need is always fuelled either by *love* or *fear*. I now understood that many of my behaviours in relationships had been based on fears which were rooted in my early years as a child and were deeply buried in my unconscious mind.

For example, since being a little girl, I learned that giving tokens of love to my mother resulted in receiving a little appreciation. Sometimes, I would pick daisies for her on the way home from school or make her a cup of tea without being asked in order to receive that one smile of gratitude. This habit of 'needing to please' continued into my adulthood and future relationships. "Giving gifts is not such a bad thing," you may quite rightly say. However, we must consider the *intention* behind the behaviour. For me, the intention was to gain some affection; to feel appreciated and loved by my mother.

Therefore, it was the *lack of something* – in this case, not getting enough love – that fuelled my motivation to give my mother gifts. In other words, underneath this drive was a deeply ingrained fear of not being loved enough. On the other hand, if I had always felt secure in the knowledge that I was loved and accepted, I might have given gifts out of a sense of generosity. The intention would, therefore, have been based on love, not fear, and a desire to simply share what I already had plenty of.

Whether it is big or small, we all have one or two fears embedded deeply in our unconscious minds, which we are usually, completely unaware of. These fears are always installed during the first five to seven years of life, when our brains are like sponges, absorbing everything around us without discernment or filters. It is usually during these all-important formative years that we develop our core beliefs about ourselves and our world.[13]

Therefore, what we believe about relationships is also programmed in at the earliest age from the environment in which we grow up. We absorb emotions, attitudes and behaviours from our immediate family, primary caregivers and teachers. If we have a good, solid foundation of feeling loved, safe and secure, we will expect to have similar standards in our future relationships. If, however, we experience traumas, hurt and hardships, especially during early childhood, we will automatically grow to feel fearful and attract similar experiences in the future.

There are also cases where people have had perfectly loving childhoods yet grown up with particular insecurities from the odd negative experience that somehow turned into fear. It simply depends on how the individual perceives a situation and processes it in his/her mind. For instance, if you were constantly told, "Oh, what a bright and clever child you are," it could turn into a fear of being different because you *think* you are more intelligent than others. However, this is not an opportunity to lay blame upon our parents, teachers or environment, but to learn to accept that we are all individual in the way we interpret our world. It is more pertinent to take responsibility for the way we *choose* to let the fears affect our relationships in our present lives.

The problem is that even if we are aware of these fears, such deeply-rooted negative thoughts and beliefs can be terribly difficult to dislodge. I like to call these fears our inner 'dragons'. These creatures reside in the deep, dark dungeons of our subconscious minds. Mostly, they like to sit in the background, watching and waiting to sabotage our best intentions. Unbeknownst to us, they will happily spend years quietly cooking up trouble down in their caves until it's time to instigate their ingenious but wicked plans to ruin our romantic lives. Then, just when we are least expecting it, they will rise from their lairs, unleash their nastiness and cause havoc.

When I mention dragons, you might be imagining a dangerous, powerful beast that breathes fire but of course, you know it is entirely mythical. So, you're probably thinking that no such dragon exists in your mind and you couldn't possibly harbour such a horrid creature. Well, don't worry – you'll be glad to know that none of us go through life without entertaining one or two of these little monsters in the dungeons of our brains. I like to think of dragons in the same manner that psychologist, Carl Jung, referred to the 'shadow' part of our psyche.[14]

In my case, my dragon was mainly one ugly fear that steered me to attract the kind of men who took my affection but were unable to give it back. I used to always, try too hard, giving away my heart too soon and never receive the same in return. I was forever hungry and wanting more love but never understanding why I didn't get it. Only once I had faced my dragon did I begin to understand its roots and was able to overcome it. Mine was a very common dragon, a hard-wired fear that makes you believe *you are not good enough*. I used to believe I was not good enough to be loved, appreciated or truly cared for. So, I named my dragon, the 'I'm Not Good Enough' dragon or 'INGE' for short (pronounced like the Scandinavian name, Inga).

So now, are you ready to face your dragon and release those deep down fears? This will require you to take a step into your 'discomfort zone'. But rest assured; it will bring about a much better emotionally healthy you and a deeper level of wellbeing. I developed the following tools for my clients and have tried and tested them with incredible results. These simple yet magical tools were initially provided by my wonderful Fae, who guided me, step-by-step, through how to apply them. They have completely changed my previous negative patterns and transformed my life. Now, I am delighted to be able to share them with you.

As with anything new, it may feel a bit awkward, silly or strange at first. However, with a little patience, you too, can find your ideal path to healing your heart and transform those negative patterns and programmes, for good. Over time, you can also adapt the tools to your individual needs by asking your own IGS.

LESSON 6: Transform Old Programmes

Do the following exercises in the order given, from A to D. This will allow your mind to get used to the process. We will be tapping into your subconscious, as that is where your dragon lives. As you become more accustomed to it, your subconscious mind will do most of the work for you. If you find yourself having to 'work at it' or think too hard, then you will only be using your conscious brain to come up with rational answers. Instead, try to relax and go with the flow.

A. Recognise Your Patterns

This exercise will help you identify your default programmes and subconscious patterns that usually dictate how you behave and the kind of behaviour you attract in others. It is best to do this exercise spontaneously without worrying too much about getting it right or wondering which situation to choose.

1. Think about all of the relationships you have had in the past, starting with the most recent first and going backwards.
2. In your notebook, take a double page and write the title, 'My Relationships' at the top.
3. Draw a few vertical lines down the pages to create some wide columns.
4. Write the name of each person with whom you have had a relationship along the top as a header for each column. You do not have to choose every relationship but perhaps only the more significant ones.
5. Look at the first name and bring to mind that relationship and remember the way it was. Think of a specific situation or issue that

happened. You can close your eyes and go through the event in your mind.

6. In the first column, write down a few notes describing that occurrence. (e.g., We received warnings about unpaid bills and argued.)
7. Below that, in the same column, list your partner's behaviours and actions during that event. (e.g., He/she was being critical and blamed me.)
8. Continue down the column and list your own thoughts, emotions and behaviours (e.g., I thought it was not my fault, felt angry, betrayed or behaved defensively.)
9. Draw a line across the column and repeat steps 5-8 with another situation or event with the same partner. You can select as many situations as you feel necessary to write about but usually, two or three different ones are enough.
10. Now, in the next column, think about another partner and relationship, then repeat steps 5-9.

Keep your notes short and simple. When you have finished writing, put your notebook aside and try not to dwell on it for a day or two before doing the next exercise. This will allow your subconscious mind to start working on it.

B. Change the Patterns

You can now start making changes to the default programmes or repeating patterns of specific behaviours that affect your relationships.

1. Open your notebook and take a fresh look at your notes from the last exercise. What do you notice? Are there any similarities between

the different events? Are there any commonalities in the behaviours of your partners?
2. Without thinking too much, write down your answers to the following questions:
   - What kinds of difficult situations often occurred in your previous relationships that were upsetting or hard to manage?
   - How did you feel, think and react during these situations?
   - After the situation was over, how did you feel, think or act?
   - What was your usual way of resolving the situation?
3. Now, you will begin to see a trend in your emotions, thoughts and behaviours. These are your default programmes or patterns. Which patterns would you consider were negative? And which ones are positive, that you wouldn't want to change?
4. Decide if any negative patterns are no longer beneficial in a relationship and which ones you might want to change. Make a list on a fresh page of your notebook. Be very specific.

Here are some examples of negative patterns that my clients identified during this exercise:

- Being afraid and not speaking up enough.
- Saying nasty things in anger I didn't mean.
- Avoiding difficult situations.
- Being overly reactive.
- Ignoring my intuition.
- Panicking and getting flustered.
- Worrying about unnecessary things.
- Accusing others without reason.
- Being overly critical.

- Being anxious all the time.
- Always giving in and being a doormat.
- Allowing others to use/hurt/offend me.
- Settling for less than I am worth.

5. Now, write down a *positive alternative statement* for each pattern you identified. These statements will become your *positive affirmations*. They usually start with 'I am' or 'I always'. Here are a few examples for the first three points above:
   - I am brave and can say what I want to say.
   - I always stop and think before I speak.
   - I am able to handle difficult situations easily.

Make sure to write the statements in the present tense and not in future tense. You can copy the most important affirmations onto sticky notes and place them where you will see them every day as you did before in Chapter 5. This will help your subconscious mind to work on making them become your reality.

You can find more useful exercises on how to recognise and change patterns in my E-book, *Am I Happy with Others?*[15]

C. Identify Your Dragon

Most probably, you are now becoming aware of the underlying reasons for the way you think and behave in a relationship. In this exercise, it is time to put down your guard, remove any façade you usually hide behind and be brutally honest with yourself.

Ask yourself the following questions and write down your answers spontaneously:

a) What one thing did you most need in those relationships?
b) Did you get what you needed?
c) How would you feel if you did get what you needed? Imagine receiving it.
d) Why is this need very important to you? What does it mean to you?
e) Looking back at all of your relationships, how often did you get what you needed?
f) At the end of each relationship, what did you think and feel?
g) When you are between relationships and single, what do you want the most?

When you have answered these questions with absolute honesty, you will have identified the thing you most need or want and the thing/quality that was lacking in your previous relationships. The deeper reason is usually quite logical and once you understand *why* you need this, you will have identified your relationship dragon. This is the fear that underlies your repeating patterns. Here are some examples of some common fears.

The fear of:

- Staying single: finding no one and ending up alone.
- The unknown: stepping out of my comfort zone.
- Being unlovable: no one can love me; I am not good enough.
- Trusting others: putting my trust in someone again and being let down.
- Trusting myself: not being able to rely on myself.
- Making a bad choice: being with someone who does not suit me.
- Judgement: if my partner is not good enough.
- Criticism: not being liked because I'm not good enough.

- Loss: losing my partner and the love I have.
- Intimacy: being vulnerable or opening up.
- Being oppressed: not having the freedom to do as I want.
- Parenthood: not coping with children/being a bad parent.
- Marriage: don't want to be tied down/ no one will marry me.

If you are still not quite sure what type of dragon you might have, don't worry. The next exercise will help you dig a little deeper to uncover it.

D. Befriend Your Dragon

This is a meditative visualisation exercise to help you climb down into the dragon's lair and befriend your little monster. In other words, you will relax deeply, so you can enter your subconscious mind, get to the root of your fear and turn it into something positive. The deeper you can relax, the easier it will be to communicate with your subconscious mind.

Again, you will use your imagination in this visualisation. Allow your mind to create whatever it wants without imposing rational ideas or trying to make the images look or be the way you *think* they should. If you have trouble 'seeing' something, let go and don't try too hard. Just allow yourself to imagine whatever comes into your perceptions and follow the words.

You will need at least an hour to do this exercise, so ensure you have a quiet space and time to relax fully. Again, it is best if you record these instructions into a voice recorder and simply listen to them through earphones. Pause between each number and after the questions when recording.

1. As before, sit or lie down and settle into a comfortable position. Allow your whole body to completely relax. Take your time.
2. Take in a long, deep breath and exhale slowly. Do this three times and hold for 3-4 seconds between the in and out breaths.
3. With each breath, release any tension in your body. Bring your attention to the different parts of your body as you allow it to relax.
4. Continue breathing normally. Imagine letting in calmness with each inward breath and letting out any worries or concerns with each outward breath.
5. If any unnecessary thoughts arise, put them inside a box labelled 'Deal with Later' in your mind. Close the box and push it aside. Take your time to simply breathe and let go.
6. Say to yourself, "I am becoming more and more relaxed. I am always in control. My mind, body and spirit are now calm, relaxed and centred."
7. Count backwards slowly from 10 to 1 in your mind and imagine going deeper and deeper. With each number, feel yourself becoming more and more relaxed.
8. As you reach number 1, imagine you are back in your favourite place outside in nature. You are walking along the beach or a path in the countryside. It is a calm day and the weather is perfect. Enjoy the scenery. Take in the views, hear the sounds and breathe in the scents around you. You are feeling completely happy and at peace being here.
9. After a while, you see ahead of you the familiar walled garden. You open the gate and walk inside, through the beautiful garden, taking in the scenery. You reach the door, go inside the house and into your special room.
10. As you enter the room, you are warmly welcomed by your IGS and exchange greetings. You both settle down on the sofa together. You

feel completely safe and at ease because you know that your IGS is taking care of you at every step.

11. Your IGS turns on the TV screen and says, "I have a film for you to see". A short film starts to play showing a difficult situation that happened in your past relationship. Allow your mind to imagine whatever comes up. As you watch the film, you are emotionally detached and can simply observe as the events unfold. You watch with interest and notice the behaviours and actions of each person involved.

12. Your IGS says, "Now, I have a special guest for you to meet," and you become aware there is another character standing inside your room also watching the film. You become aware that this is your dragon. Imagine how it looks, its shape and its demeanour. The dragon is wearing a smug smile as it watches the film and seems pleased that things are going wrong in the relationship.

13. Then, the dragon notices you and comes a little closer. You and your IGS stand up to greet your dragon. The dragon is not ferocious or frightening as you might have expected. In fact, it is calm, collected and seems quite intelligent. It greets you with a wide grin. You feel at ease being in the same room with your dragon.

14. Now, you can now talk to it. Thank the dragon for joining you and ask the dragon its name.

15. Ask the dragon questions about the film on the screen. (e.g., Why did this difficult situation happen in my previous relationship? What was the real reason behind it?)

16. Allow any thoughts or words to come to mind. Mentally note any answers you receive. Do not argue with the dragon.

17. The three of you continue to watch the film until it ends. Take your time.

18. Then, ask your dragon the following questions and accept any response or reaction that comes into your awareness:

- Why did you allow things to go wrong or become difficult?
- What was the lesson I needed to learn?
- Why did I need to learn this?
- What is it I fear most?
- What was the main purpose of that relationship?

Take your time to listen and allow the dragon to reply. Accept whatever answers the dragon says in response. Thank the dragon for answering you.

19. Now, ask your dragon if it will kindly help you grow and heal: "Please, will you be my friend now? And show me what I must learn and how to change?" Imagine the dragon agreeing happily and changing into a friendly dragon. You might see it change colour, shape or expression, or it may simply give you the feeling that it has become friendlier.

20. Say thanks again and goodbye to the dragon. Watch it leave through another door.

21. You can now talk with your IGS about the dragon's lesson and ask for any further advice. Ask open questions and allow your mind to receive any ideas or thoughts that might appear.

22. Finally, say goodbye to your IGS and leave your special room.

23. Take your time to come out of this meditation. Leave the house and go back into the garden, then return along the path on which you came.

24. As you walk back, count slowly from 1 – 10 and feel yourself becoming more awake with each number.

25. Take a deep breath, let go of all your thoughts and return to the present. Open your eyes and have a good stretch.

Whilst it is still fresh in your memory, make notes of all that you saw, heard, felt and learnt during the visualisation in your notebook.

You will only need to do the meditation once but ensure you do it thoroughly. However, you can repeat it for each previous relationship, if you need to. Just remember that the dragon only needs to change into the friendly dragon once. Thereafter, you should see it only as a friendly dragon and be able to discuss your fears whenever you feel the need. You can do this by going to your special room in your mind and requesting the presence of your dragon. Then, simply talk with it in the same way as you do with your IGS.

This meditation exercise can be quite emotional and cathartic for some people. For others, it may feel like they have learned nothing new and always known the truth. This is a powerful way of accessing your subconscious mind and as you practice more, you will release yourself from the fears that once held you down. Most people will say that they can never be completely rid of their dragon but by doing this exercise it will loosen its grip on those subconscious programmes. Therefore, I recommend we practice making friends with the creature instead of trying to eliminate it.

Once you have overcome that first hurdle and confronted your dragon, the rest will get easier. You can meet with your dragon as often as you wish and discuss the reasons behind any patterns of thought, behaviour or negative tendencies. It is not always necessary for you to understand the root cause of the fear and why it was installed in the first place and that will depend on your particular experience. However, it is more important to ask the dragon and your IGS for help to change any programmes that no longer serve you.

As you face your fears, you will grow in understanding of your toughest challenges. You will learn to embrace the dragon and as you do so, it will automatically start to release its hold on you. The greatest hurdle in this part of your healing journey is in recognising that something *deep inside you* needs to change in order to reset the dial and attract the right kind of energy to you.

For me, the best part of this lesson was learning to accept that I was not at fault and stop blaming myself. Those default programmes were not my own and I did not consciously make myself behave the way I did in my past relationships. They were all learned behaviours and coping strategies which were learnt during my early childhood years. Being able to understand my deep rooted fears, default programmes and motivations was a huge step in healing my past. The next Lesson took me even farther in releasing those unhealthy ties and move towards a profound inner awareness and self-appreciation.

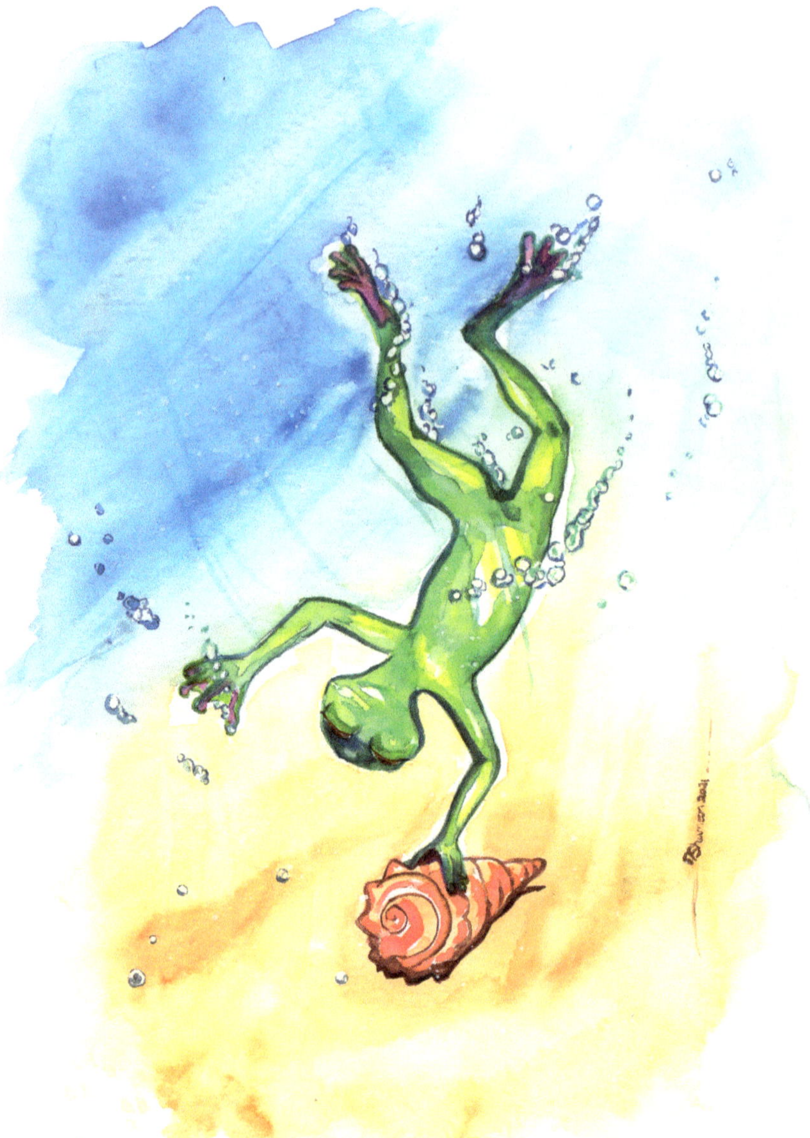

8. Breaking the Curse

"Oh, you are quite bothersome, princess," groaned the dragon, rolling over sleepily. "Whatever are you doing now?"
"Well, someone ought to clean up around here!" she complained. "There's a horrid smell and it's such a mess down here." She continued sweeping and tidying until the place looked somewhat respectable. All that remained was the dragon's untidy bed. "Do get up, Dragon," she said, pushing him with her broom.

"There's nothing here for you to clean," he said, curling up again. But before he knew it, she whipped off his blanket and prodded him again. He was startled and jumped up, trying to hide something behind his back.
"What's that?" she said curiously, trying to peer behind him.
"Nothing," replied the dragon looking guilty.

In a flash, she turned her broom around and poked his arm with the stick end. The dragon squealed and something heavy fell to the floor with a thud. There, covered in dirt, lay a small wooden chest with an engraving on its lid. "Oh, my – it has my name carved on it!" exclaimed the princess.

A True Prince

Over a year had passed since Dan and I had gone our separate ways. Slowly and carefully, I had put the pieces of my broken heart back together and regained some emotional balance. This time, I had a really good feeling that things would be different. The studies were going well at University. I was about to begin my third year and had a fairly good idea about where my new career was headed Life was good. There was no hurry but I was more than ready and open to finding my true, spiritual life partner. It was time to find a grown-up man, not another Peter Pan. I needed someone who would be on my wavelength, someone I could really talk with: a man who would be my equal, confident about who he was and where he was going.

Bob was a gentleman with all the right credentials. He worked in the city and was divorced. He was well-mannered, calm, collected and sincere. We first met at a mutual friend's home and I think we must have felt an instant connection because his eyes lit up when he spoke to me. Upon introduction, we clicked easily but he did not initiate anything until several months later when we met again in our local club. It was a delight to meet a man who seemed interesting, intelligent and who equally enjoyed music and dancing.

Before the end of the evening, he approached me quite unexpectedly and very timidly but eloquently, asked me for a date. Obviously, he had given it a lot of thought and had to muster up the courage before approaching me. I was very flattered and graciously accepted. He could hardly contain his joy as a huge smile spread across his face and he asked if we could meet the very next day.

We met at an understated bistro bar and, as it was a Sunday evening, we agreed to keep it short and just have one coffee together. However, the conversation flowed easily with this very likeable man and the hours rolled by. I was aware that Bob was talking profusely, trying hard to impress me. Then, without prompting, he apologised for rambling on and asked questions about me, listening intently. His nervousness was rather charming and I remember thinking how witty, honest and wise he was. This was a man who genuinely had no false pretences and no need to be anything other than his true self. I was duly impressed.

"What an attractive, handsome man he is," I thought, as he was speaking, noticing his natural masculinity and smart dress sense. And at the same time, a tiny little gut feeling rose up from somewhere deep inside, saying, "But you don't actually *feel* any attraction to him, do you?" It was that quiet little voice of Fae whispering again, worming her way into my thoughts and spoiling the moment.

"Oh, don't be silly!" I said to myself, brushing away the little worm and persuading myself otherwise. "Come on girl, grow up! You know that 'chemistry' is well over-rated. Isn't it time you changed your tune and allowed a different kind of man into your life?" Yes, indeed, it was time for a new strategy.

It wasn't until many years later, when I had nurtured my relationship enough with Fae to know how she operated, that I fully understood how to recognise that little whisper. With Bob, I put it down to a lack of chemistry but of course it was much more than that. It was my all-knowing, intuitive self trying to warn me, with the aid of my physical senses, that my feelings at the very beginning of any relationship should not be ignored.

Alas, it was easy to ignore that gut feeling with Bob. Until then, apart from my father, he was the kindest, most caring and considerate man that I had ever met. He did his utmost to give with all his heart, be attentive and treat me like a lady. Despite having had two children with his first wife, and not wanting anymore, he was still willing to reverse the vasectomy for me. "How incredibly benevolent," I thought. "It is a privilege to be loved by this man – why shouldn't I love him back?" It was as though the gods were, at last, blessing me with the kind of love I thought I deserved. Finally, the old curses had been broken. He must be the answer to my heart's longing.

Bob always had a busy schedule, working long hours, commuting into the city every day, as well as fishing, golfing and having his kids stay over at the weekends. This was not a problem for me as I too, was very busy with my studies. So, we made the best of our quality time together during the evenings and weekends. Being with Bob was so comfortable and uncomplicated.

Whist I was obliviously enjoying my new relationship, Inge was brewing up some other devious plans. As the months rolled by, little niggling doubts started to creep in and pester my conscious thoughts. I found myself being irritated by Bob for no apparent reason. After some time, the things that had once been endearing about him became annoying. He would do nothing that was terribly wrong but invariably, I found myself complaining. My own behaviour then became a source of further frustration and I would get cross with myself for being annoyed at him. "What on earth is wrong with me?!" I berated myself but had no explanation.

We went on a long-awaited summer holiday together and I had hoped it would help us get back to being happy together. But, as I'm sure you know, if a couple already has underlying relationship issues, spending concentrated time together only brings the problems up to the surface. One day, I made a scathing and uncalled for remark at Bob. Realising just how unkind I could be to him, and hating myself for it, I decided that things must change.

After the holiday, I analysed my own behaviour and the truth began to dawn upon me. I remember driving home from college one evening and thinking, "I haven't seen him for days but that's okay. I'm not really missing him. In fact, I'm quite happy if we can both do our own thing this weekend. I've got so much studying to do anyway". Of course, having time apart should be fine. We all know that giving each other space is good and healthy in an adult relationship.

I thought a lot about my awful comments over the last several months and realised just how lucky I was because Bob was always so tolerant and never retaliated whenever I snapped at him. "He is a much better human being than you," I scolded myself. "He would be so much better off with someone who is more 'earthy', like himself and not so feisty, like you." I imagined him with someone like a nurse or a carer on his arm, both looking very happy together. "Yes, a person who has a kindly soul, is more tolerant, easy-going and less irritable would suit him perfectly. I wonder if I could change and be that person? Perhaps, I don't deserve to be with him, not the way I treat him."

As I drove into my parking space pondering these thoughts, that little voice, instead of whispering, shouted at me, sending an alarm bell ringing in my head! I turned off the engine and sat staring blankly into space, dumbstruck by my own bizarre train of thought. "Hello, is that really you? What the heck is wrong with you?! This is not the woman I know *you* to be!" I said to myself in shock. "How can you even entertain the thought of *your man* being with another woman? If you truly loved him, you would never think *that* way about him. Remember how possessive you are? Wake up and smell the facts!"

There it was, the brutal truth staring me in the face. "How could I have been so blind? Here I am making excuses to not spend time with Bob and actually *imagining* him being with someone else," I thought. "How could I possibly be *in love* with him, if I can have such thoughts? And if I am always snapping at him for no good reason, what does that say about my *actual* feelings for him?" It began to dawn on me that my aggravating behaviour towards Bob was being steered by my subconscious mind because, no matter how much I consciously wanted to be nice to him, I was still automatically getting annoyed. The cold hard truth was that underneath it all, I was annoyed at myself.

I finally realised that my irritability at Bob had little to do with him and everything to do with my own sense of lack. I loved him, yes, but not... well, not wholly. Not the way I knew myself to be capable of loving someone. Whatever it was that I was feeling for Bob, it was certainly not the kind of love he truly deserved. And sadly, it was not the kind of absolute love that he felt for me. I realised that, underneath those sharp comments, I was harbouring guilt, disappointment and anger at myself because I couldn't feel the same way towards him. What I was certain of was that he deserved to be appreciated and accepted for being himself, just the way he was, and to be loved so much more than I was able to.

Once again, I was engulfed in more heartbreak. Bob was gentle and understanding as always. He didn't blame me or show any reproach when I explained how I felt. "I already knew," he said sadly. "Your heart was never meant for me." We said our goodbyes and were both utterly miserable. I knew I had wounded him badly. I could have taken the easy route and stayed but I had to do what was right for both of us.

As ever, I went home, took refuge inside my shell and scrutinised every piece of the broken relationship. I vented my frustrations in my notebooks and complained to Fae: "You said to keep an open mind and I did! That's why I ignored the tiny voice when I first met him. I thought it was just my silly fears trying to sabotage my chances." It was incredibly frustrating. I felt thoroughly disappointed with myself and very sad for Bob. "So, tell me: where did I go wrong? Where does all this stupid, antagonistic behaviour come from? Is it because of my childhood? Should I blame my parents? How am I supposed to change this awful default programme?"

There were so many unanswered questions and Fae wasn't very clear either. Even if I received answers, I did not have any idea how to go about changing my patterns or programmes. At the time, I was still learning how to change my limited thinking and I was still a long way from meeting my dragon. As usual, I just wanted to learn the lesson and move on. My impatience with myself had always pushed me to race ahead without giving myself enough time to properly reflect and heal.

At least I learned one important lesson: if we get overly emotional and our reactions are disproportionate to the given situation, it is always because of a deeper issue that needs to be addressed. Usually, it is some underlying hurt, sadness or fear which is trying to express itself. We don't notice them because we tend to focus only on the foolish surface behaviours that happen in relationships. However, dragons do what they do for a very good reason. Their main purpose for existing in the dungeons of our psyche is actually, not because they want to be malevolent. They have an ulterior motive, which is to make you face your deepest wounds and overcome your hidden fears. This is its main intention: to help you learn, heal and transcend those ingrained fears.

Treasure Chests

The princess felt she had made little progress on her journey and locked herself away in her lonely tower for a while. "No chance of encountering any unworthy toads up here," she decided, but she had yet to learn her greatest lesson. *The gods had decided that in order to accomplish her mission, she must first sink to the depths of the murkiest quagmire of misery with nowhere to go other than face her evil dragon. Only then, after shedding more unnecessary layers, would she discover the true, authentic princess and be able to continue on her quest in finding true love.*

After the relationship with Bob came to an end, I remained single for several years, struggling with my inner healing and trying to take on board the many lessons I'd been given. I knew it was something to do with my default programmes but was still unsure as to what exactly those negative beliefs were. They were so difficult to reach and lay deeply entrenched in my social conditioning and enforced cultural values. Unfortunately, it would take a couple more disastrous relationships before I could finally face the wounds of my past and pull out the roots of those reoccurring patterns.

One evening, during the months of grieving following the wrath of Rick (Chapter Three), I was doing my usual meditation and went to my special room. As always, I was warmly greeted by Fae and she seemed unusually excited to see me. "I have something very important and valuable for you," she said, gesturing that I follow her out of the room and go through a different door, one I had not noticed before. We went past a courtyard and along a dark corridor.

"Where are we going?" I asked. This was all very new to me.
"Come on; you'll see," she urged.

I followed her down some winding steps and through another door which opened into a dark, mysterious room. "This must be the dungeon of my castle," I thought. I looked around and could see nothing except for three old wooden chests lying on the floor. "Is this supposed to be treasure?" I asked, feeling amused by my own imagination.

Fae just smiled and indicated that I should look inside. As I moved closer, I noticed that each chest had a label. The first said 'Partners', the second said 'Mother' and the third I couldn't quite make out as it was in the dark.

"We will open these in due course and work through them," said Fae. "Now, open the first one," she said, handing me a key. My clever, creative brain had obviously gone into overdrive, I thought. So, I played along with the whimsical nonsense that was unfolding. By now, I had learned that at this creative level of the mind, it is better to just go with the flow and try not to make logical sense of anything.

I knelt down in front of the first chest and opened it carefully. Inside, it was filled with gold and jewels. "Hmm... seriously?" I raised my eyebrows at Fae, thinking this was getting ridiculous and that maybe, I'd been watching too many pirate movies.
"This is all yours," she said, "but that's not the real treasure. Look underneath."

I started pulling out handfuls of gold coins and jewellery, letting the treasure spill across the floor. Buried at the bottom, I found some small paper cards, each with something written on them. Although I couldn't make out the text, I knew that each card represented a different relationship from my past. I turned to Fae, holding out the cards and asking her what they were for. Now, I began to feel intrigued and thought perhaps, this was not complete nonsense after all.

"You must forgive each one of them," said Fae.

"But I thought I had done all that, years ago… didn't I?" I asked, trying to recall some distant archived memories.

"You must write a letter to each person and forgive each one," she clarified.

As soon as she'd said this, the words I needed to write started to stream into my thoughts. They were very precise and poured into my mind as though I were receiving a 'download' of information.

In the next instant, we were outside, standing on the shore of a broad, sandy beach. In front of us, there stood an empty oil drum which was charred black from being used for burning. Fae then indicated one of the cards in my hand and said, "Read the card. You must *feel* it."

I did as she instructed, and as I was about to read the card, all the feelings I once felt for my ex rose up again inside me, feelings of deep sorrow, frustration and guilt. "Now, take out those feelings and burn them," said Fae. I saw a thick, dark cloud emerging from somewhere inside my belly area. I imagined its heaviness as I pulled it out with both hands and felt it leave my body. Then, I hurled the pile into the drum. With a match, I set light to the ghastly mass. It immediately caught on fire and I watched the flames consume it, transforming it into a thick, gloopy, tar-like substance. It burned brightly, then melted down until it disintegrated into a small pile of feather-light ashes. Finally, a big wave rolled in, washing over it all, sweeping everything away, leaving just the empty drum.

"Good," said Fae. I was astounded by the scenes I had just seen and looked at her, incredulous and unable to speak. After this vivid and powerful experience, I thought I should be feeling some kind of profound change within, but somehow, nothing particular seemed to be different.

I guessed I would have to be patient and wait for the experience to take effect.

"Now, go and do this for real," said Fae. I instantly understood her instructions. I would have to write a card for each and every relationship from my past and then burn them in real life. "And don't forget to say, 'I forgive you'," she added.
"Thank you so much for showing me all this and guiding me. And thank you for always taking care of me," I said and bid her farewell. I was left feeling a curious mixture of relief and reluctance as I came back out of my meditation.

I had often been guided to do practical tasks by Fae before and they never failed. It was just a matter of trusting the process. However, this one seemed like a real chore and not much fun at all. The next day, I noted down all the instructions she had given me and wondered if there was any point to such a lengthy task. I didn't want to spend hours writing stuff on paper that I would have to *burn*. After all, I was used to keeping all of my written notes and journals. This seemed like a crazy idea and I knew I was resisting doing it.

The next night, Fae appeared again and asked why I had not done the exercise. "I'm still not sure how it can help," I admitted.
"Just trust," was her simple reply.
"Hmm... yes, okay, I'll do it at the weekend," I promised. Then, as I let go and relaxed into my meditation space, I received the next download of words about another relationship. It was as if Fae wanted to ensure that I understood exactly what I had to do. Soon, my barriers fell away and I allowed myself to simply accept all that I was being given. Again, I was awestruck by the whole experience and how it was filled with much gentleness, understanding and compassion throughout.

That Sunday, I found some old blank index cards and started to write the letters. I started with the most recent relationship as it was still fresh in my mind:

Dear Rick

Thank you for coming into my life and the relationship we once had. You shared your heart, mind and inner self with me. I don't know if you actually loved me but thank you for trying. You also shared your pain and anger and vented your frustrations on me. I had to walk on eggshells around you because you were often nasty and hurtful to me.

I gave you all my heart, love and friendship. I shared my soul, my hopes and dreams, my whole self with you. I was always the one driving all the way to your place, bringing you gifts and making time to be with you. I was ready to share my life with you. In return, you were selfish and distrusting. You assumed things about me that were untrue and ignored what I wanted. I did nothing to deserve this behaviour from you. When you let me go, you hurt me so terribly it tore my heart apart. But I understand that you had many troubles and could not control your outbursts. I know inside, you were suffering from past relationships and traumas. But they were your traumas which had nothing to do with me.

Now, I forgive you for all that you did to me. I forgive your nasty behaviours and inability to love me as I am. I let go of all attachment to you and release any feelings I might have held for you. I wish you well and release you from my heart with love. Goodbye.

Surprisingly, the letter was not as long or as difficult to write as I had expected. I got myself a cup of tea and continued with the rest of the cards. Remembering those relationships brought up tears as I wrote and I swallowed down the lump in my throat every time. The hardest one to write was for Bob. There was nothing to forgive but luckily, Fae had given me the words I needed to say:

Dear Bob

Thank you for coming into my life and giving me so much love. You were always so kind, caring and understanding. You gave me all of your heart and loyalty. I am terribly sorry for all the nasty things I said and giving you a hard time when you really didn't deserve it. It was hard but in the end, I am glad we parted because I knew I could never give you the same kind of love in return.

Because of you, I learned to face the truth and be really honest with myself. You showed me how to be a better human being and be more compassionate. Thank you. You proved to me that there really are genuine, reliable, good men out there. You restored my faith in knowing that a good relationship with a deeper connection is possible.

I have nothing to forgive you for but I now forgive myself for hurting you and let go of all the sadness and guilt. I release all attachment to you and let go of any feelings I might still be holding. I wish you all the happiness you truly deserve and release you from my heart with love.

Soon, all the cards were written and laid out on my desk. I was now ready for the next part, and later that evening when all was quiet, just before dusk, I stepped out into my garden. Despite feeling a bit silly, I stood in front of the old barbeque grill, a lighter in my hand, ready to do the burning exercise. There was a slight chill in the air and I stared up at the sky. "Well, I'm doing as I was told, I am trusting. I don't know if this is going to do any good but here goes," I said in my mind to Fae.

I took out the first card from my pocket and read it slowly, allowing myself to feel all the emotions it provoked about that relationship. Again, I emphasised the final words of forgiveness as I placed the card on the grill, took a deep breath and lit it. Instantly, the little flame caught the paper card, burning it up easily. The fire grew bigger before shrinking and dying down. As I watched each card burn, I acknowledged each and every soul, including their friends and families who had been a part of my life during our relationship, and said goodbye to them all. I felt a sense of closure, like the sadness of loss and letting go.

As I finished burning the last card, I remembered that not so long ago, I had stood in this same spot, in my garden and cried out to the gods to make things right. "Wow! Maybe they heard me. Maybe this might just work."

Thinking about those relationships, one by one, and remembering all that I had been through was a very emotional experience. But it was also a very necessary cathartic and healing one. Although, at first, I did not notice any great changes in myself, I was glad that I had completed the exercise.

Only after several months did I truly understand the powerful benefits and freedom it had given me. The burning exercise had broken the curse and freed me of all those negative emotional attachments and my old desperate, needy hunger for love. Interestingly, within a matter of weeks, I started coming out of the tunnel of darkness and the tears of grief soon dried up.

Unchaining Myself

At last, I found myself beginning to feel lighter, happier and more relaxed inside as I continued to follow the directions given by Fae. After I had forgiven all of my exes, I was able to take the next, most crucial step: to forgive myself. For most of us, this is probably the most challenging part of all. A few years later, I was guided to open the other trunks and rewrite the other long-held default programmes installed in me as a child.

At first, when I pulled out this card from the trunk, I really didn't understand why I should need to forgive myself. The concept of self-forgiveness was rather alien to me. After all, what had I done that had been so wrong? Was it such a bad idea to get married to Ted? Did I do something terrible to Dan? Hadn't I always given my absolute best and poured as much love as possible into every relationship?

As always, with kind and gentle instruction, Fae guided me during my meditations. Whilst in my special room, she told me to imagine seeing me from outside of myself, through the eyes of a beloved person. This meant that I had to step outside of myself and imagine that a good friend was standing in front of me and talking to me. So, I chose my dear old friend Cherie, stepped into her shoes, and imagined looking at me through her eyes. Instantly, the things she would most likely think and say became perfectly clear in my head.

I repeated this exercise a couple more times with another friend and a caring relative. The results were, needless to say, astonishing to me. I felt and heard my dear ones express emotions and words such as:

- You did nothing wrong in trying to love Bob.
- You did everything you could to make that relationship work. And that was enough.

- You are still lovable, even when you think you've done something wrong.
- It is not a mistake to have loved someone completely, even if he could not love you back.
- Forgive yourself for always trying to please your parents and partners.
- Forgive yourself for always trying so hard to get things right and being tough on yourself.
- Forgive yourself for thinking you are inferior and lowering your standards.
- Forgive yourself for believing you lack something.
- Forgive yourself for thinking that no one will love you as you are.
- Forgive yourself for the things you did in the past when you didn't know better.

Slowly but surely, I came face-to-face with the deep-down limiting thoughts and beliefs that I had been unaware of, which had always influenced the way I felt about myself. I began to uncover the seeds that were planted in the distant past and pull out the weeds from their roots. Once upon a time, they served me well but now they had become burdens and untruths that I no longer needed to carry. Finally, this exercise released me from the chains that had invisibly bound me to those old, outworn thoughts, expectations and motivations, for good.

Forgiving myself was essential in becoming a better version of who I am, my true and authentic self. Only then, could I move towards having more genuine, natural and balanced relationships with others.

Forgiveness

Before we go any further, I must clarify one crucial factor that needs to be understood. When I mentioned forgiving my ex, what came to mind when you thought about 'forgiveness'? How would you feel if you were to do the same? Does it conjure up thoughts of letting the other person 'off the hook', that you would be allowing him or her to get away with what she/he did? Does it upset you because it feels as though you will have to forget, accept or 'bow down' to all that had gone wrong?

According to the dictionary, to forgive means to 'stop feeling angry or resentful towards [someone] for an offence, flaw, or mistake' and to 'no longer wish to punish them'.[16] Therefore, forgiveness does not mean to pardon, permit or agree with the other person's wrong doings. In fact, it is not about them at all; it is about *you*. In other words, forgiveness means to stop the bad feelings you have towards the other person and let go of whatever you are holding against them.

Also, forgiveness does not necessarily mean we should forget. How can we forget some of the most difficult and painful episodes of our lives? It is rather unrealistic to do so. Moreover, if we did forget it all, how would we learn from those experiences? When you forgive someone for what they have done, you can stop dwelling on that distressing experience and allowing it to continue harming your life. Once you can accept that it is healthier to let go, you can work on purging the pain and put the last remnants away in the memory archives of your mind. Only then will you be able to move on with your life and be free of carrying that baggage into your next relationship.

Therefore, when we change our perspective of what 'forgiving your ex' actually means, the process becomes much easier. I suggest thinking of it as 'freeing your heart', and thus, liberating your mind, body and soul from all that negative energy.

The real test for knowing whether you have completely forgiven someone is when you no longer feel anything bad or get upset whenever you think of her/him again. Instead, you feel neutral towards your ex and you do not get emotional when you talk about him/her. It should be similar to the kind of 'non-feeling' you have towards an old acquaintance or distant friend who you once knew but is now no longer a part of your life.

Before you do the following exercises, imagine being unbound and having freedom from all that once troubled and hurt you. These exercises will stop those negative cycles and break the chains that kept cursing every new relationship. You may not notice the difference at first, but once you have done the tasks, your subconscious mind will assimilate the new programmes and release those old unconscious, negative patterns. Eventually, when you are ready, you will be unencumbered and able to love completely and whole-heartedly again without the dragon's influence.

LESSON 7: Free Your Heart

A. Forgive the Ex

This exercise will help you release any attachments you may unknowingly be harbouring such as hurt, resentment, guilt, shame or a grudge towards your ex. It is worthwhile doing this exercise even if you think there is nothing to forgive as there might still be some long-forgotten emotional baggage trapped deep inside your subconscious mind.

You will need a pen and some plain pieces of paper or card to write on. Allow enough time to do the exercise and ensure that you are alone and undisturbed.

1. Write a short letter to each ex-partner from your past on separate pieces of paper. If you are unsure whether the relationship was significant or not, ask yourself if you still get upset or annoyed when you think of that person. If so, go ahead and write a letter to her/him.
2. Your letter should include the following points:
    - name of person to whom you are writing
    - acknowledge your ex-partner and give him/her thanks for coming into your life
    - describe the relationship very briefly
    - state how her/his actions and behaviours affected you
    - state your feelings, needs or thoughts about the relationship
    - anything you want to say that you've never had the chance to say before
    - finish by saying, 'I forgive you completely and release you with love.'

3. Take your letters to a place, preferably outside, where you can burn them safely. Be careful if there is windy weather. Allow for smoke and ensure you do this away from any other flammable materials.

4. Give yourself time to read each letter and think about that relationship. Allow any emotions to arise and do not rush this part. You can also close your eyes, imagine your ex in front of you and tell him/her anything else that you need to say.

5. Now, let them go – imagine her/him wrapped in love and walking away from you, getting smaller and disappearing into the distance. Firmly, say the words of forgiveness aloud and feel the emotions of absolute release.

6. Burn the letter very carefully and feel all your emotions or any remaining attachments burn away with the flames.

After you have finished burning all the pieces of paper, you can place the cooled ashes on the earth and imagine them dissolving into the ground, being neutralised. You may wish to sprinkle the ashes with water to ensure there are no embers left.

B. Have Your Say

This is an optional visualisation exercise which will allow you to express and release any feelings, good or bad, about your past relationships. You will be able to talk with your ex-partner about anything that might have been left unsaid and finally, close the door.

You must approach this exercise with an open mind and put down your sword and shield. In this virtual world, there is no need for attack or defence. You can just be your authentic, vulnerable self. You can use this method for your ex or on any other close relationship that needs closure.

As with the previous meditation exercises, I recommend that you read the following directions into a voice recorder, ensuring that you pause between each number. Then, simply listen to the recording and do the exercise.

1. As always, start by relaxing your mind and body. Settle down into a comfortable position and close your eyes.
2. Take three long, deep breaths. Focus on the different parts of your body and relax as you let go of any tension.
3. Allow your mind to relax as you count from 10 to 1 slowly. As before, imagine you are taking a walk outside in your peaceful place. Take your time to enjoy the scenery and notice your surroundings using all of your senses.
4. Walk along the path until you get to the gate and go through into the beautiful garden. Then, enter the house and go to your special room.
5. Imagine switching on the TV screen and a film of your previous relationship starts to play. You see your ex-partner doing something, just as she/he always used to do.
6. Now, see him/her turn to face you and then step out of the screen. She/he is now standing in front of you, with a neutral expression. Imagine you are talking with him/her, and he/she is willingly listening. You can now tell her/him anything you want or that you might have always wanted to say. Be honest and feel free to express yourself fully.
7. Then, ask your ex if there is anything she/he wants to say. Let him/her speak and listen calmly without interrupting. Do not argue and allow your ex to have his/her say. When she/he has finished, give your thanks.
8. Now, imagine your ex is calmly listening to you. From the following statements, select one that is most appropriate and fill in the blanks

with your own words. Or create your own statement of forgiveness. Say these words to her/him with feeling:

- I now forgive you for the way you behaved/treated me and for... (*whatever they did that was bad*). These things no longer bother me. I release all bad feelings that I might have had and you do not have any effect on me anymore. I let go of all emotions towards you.

- I am truly sorry and I regret that... (*whatever you did that you feel bad about*). Please forgive me for the way I treated you. I now let go of all these feelings and no longer allow them to affect me. I release myself from any guilt or shame I might have had held onto.

9. See your ex accepting your words and thank him/her for listening. Imagine all that happened in the past is now completely released for both of you. See her/him wrapped in a brilliant light of love and positive energy. You may want to wish him/her well for their future before you finally, say goodbye.

10. Watch him/her turn around, go back into the screen and disappear through a door in the distance. Imagine all your attachments or emotions to that relationship leaving and disappearing with them.

11. You are now enjoying a feeling of release, calm and lightness surrounding you. Feel glad and grateful that this is now done and the door is firmly closed on that relationship.

12. Take a long, deep, cleansing breath and as you breathe out, blow away all the images and emotions from this exercise. You have now let go of it all and are completely free.

13. Come out of this meditation as you have done before, taking your time. Count slowly back from 1 to 10 and feel becoming lighter and more awake with each number. Open your eyes when you are ready and have a good stretch.

C. Forgive Yourself

This exercise is essential for healing your heart and I recommend it to everyone. It will help you release any buried negative emotions that you, knowingly or unknowingly, might still be holding onto. These emotions could be related to any previous relationship, childhood programmes or difficult experiences you might have had in the past.

For instance, when we get angry and continue to stay upset with the other person, perhaps longer than necessary, it is an indication of being angry at ourselves. Quite often, we unknowingly harbour these kind of negative feelings towards ourselves and cannot find a way to release them. With this exercise, you will unload such toxic emotions, thoughts and beliefs so you can clear your heart for healthier self-love.

As you did before in Chapter Five, this is another mirror exercise you can do in your bathroom.

1. First, sit down for a moment, take a deep breath and close your eyes. Relax into your thoughts.
2. Bring to mind a good friend or relative who knows and loves you deeply. Imagine you are now that person: step into their mind and hear their thoughts. Feel the feelings they have for you and imagine looking at yourself through her/his loving eyes.
3. As you do this, spontaneous ideas, thoughts or feelings should come into your mind. If not, imagine that person thinking about you and asking this question; "What quality do you not acknowledge about yourself?" Listen to any answers that arise.
4. Thank your friend or relative and come back into yourself and your own mind. Open your eyes. Take these thoughts from your friend and use them for the next steps.

5. Now, stand in front of your mirror and take another deep breath.
6. Look deep into your own eyes and say the following aloud. Select the statements and words that you feel are most appropriate and fill in the blanks accordingly:
    - I forgive you for thinking you were not good enough.
    - I forgive you for being angry/jealous/sad... about...
    - I love you and completely forgive you for... (actions, thoughts or feelings).
    - I forgive you for not letting go of... before now.
    - I forgive you for all the times you ignored your own needs.
    - I forgive you for acting out patterns of behaviour you learned in childhood.
    - You did the best you could with the skills, knowledge and experience you had at that time. Now, you now know better and you are doing better.
7. Take your time and feel the emotions of the words as you are saying them. Do not look away from your own eyes as you say the words to your reflection. Allow any thoughts and feelings to arise and acknowledge them.
8. Take a long, deep breath and let it all go.
9. Optional step: have a wash or shower and imagine the water cleansing away those old feelings that no longer serve you.

These are just some examples of self-forgiveness statements but you can also adapt or create your own. This is a very personal experience and it is essential that you are brutally honest with yourself.

I recommend that you repeat the exercise every day, for at least seven days, but you can continue for as long as you feel necessary. At first, it may feel strange and you'll find excuses to resist doing it. It might make you feel rather uncomfortable or your mind may wander during the exercise. There is also a chance that hidden issues will arise that you have not yet considered. This is all quite normal and to be expected, so push through the resistance and do it anyway.

Allow yourself time to go through the process and let your heart release all the feelings you've been holding onto. After you have done the mirror exercise a few times, you will no longer need to imagine a friend telling you about your qualities. Over time, I promise it will get easier and you will start to feel lighter inside. Slowly, you will create the emotional space to free your heart and welcome a new love.

When I first did this exercise, I was overwhelmed with sadness and empathy for the woman in the mirror. However, after doing the exercises, my self-awareness grew tremendously and I felt happier, telling myself what I really needed to hear.

One of the greatest realisations I had was to understand and forgive my mother. Her reasons for insisting I marry Ted became clear to me and I was able to remove some deep-seated resentful feelings towards her. At the time of the ceremony, I had assumed she was being selfish and only cared about what other people thought. I have since realised that she was doing her best to keep me safe, ensure that I didn't get into trouble, as she had at my age, and avoid becoming an outcast. She was operating from a very old programme which was not her fault but the result of her social conditioning. Her beliefs were steeped in antiquated traditions and a lack of knowledge. This steered her actions which sadly, were also affected by a mountain of emotional baggage that she was never able to release.

Accepting my mother as she was allowed me the freedom, not only to forgive her, but also to let go of any self-resentment I might have had about my own involvement in allowing the marriage. I was only 25 back then, and had experienced very little of life. I lacked self-worth and the courage to stand up for myself. After the exercises, I was able to appreciate that I had done the best I could, given the circumstances I was in, at that time. Hence, my self-forgiveness was absolutely necessary to stop being hard on myself and heal my past.

The relationship with Bob and subsequent break-up also began to make sense. I realised that I had not chosen whether or not to fall in love with him. Yes, it had been my choice to be with him and I was responsible for that. It was a decision I had made with my head, not my heart, soul and whole being. Many years later, I learned that real love for another person is not something we can *make* happen. Genuine, true love between two people is a feeling that happens naturally, and it either exists, or it doesn't.

Several years later, I saw Bob again at a social gathering and he was with his new girlfriend. I was really pleased to see that they seemed to be very happy together. Interestingly, she was indeed, a kindly, gentle and beautiful soul whose profession was a nurse.

Learning to forgive has taught me one of the most valuable lessons in life. I have always thought of myself as a person who never holds onto guilt, grudges or spite towards anyone. It is not in my nature to stay angry or feel resentful to others for long. Yet, I still needed to learn how to forgive previous partners and release myself from those relationships, not because of any nasty feelings I had, but in order to stop the unconscious negative programmes from continuing to sabotage my future. Forgiving myself and the past cleared the space in my heart and stopped the old patterns so that I could attract much happier and healthier relationships.

9. Weaving a Magic Spell

The princess toyed with her crown, fingering the decorative edges and thought, "It can't really have any magical powers, can it?"
Owl scratched her head, wondering how she might explain it better to her student. "Do try again," she urged gently. "And remember, you must believe."

The princess was getting tired but did as she was told. Putting her crown back on, she closed her eyes tightly and took a deep breath. She tapped the crown three times with her wand whilst saying the magic words.

Owl watched her closely, then abruptly, stopped the poor princess mid-sentence. "Why are you frowning, my girl?" she said, shaking her head.
"Because I am trying hard to concentrate," replied the princess, rather exasperated. "Oh, boo! I'll never learn how to do real magic."

Owl was pensive for a while. "Ho-hum, never mind. That'll be enough for today," she said, sighing. "You can stop trying now. Just think about your favourite flowers instead."

The princess smiled with relief. As she remembered the blooms in her garden, suddenly, a tingle shot up her spine, through her head and gave her goose bumps. Just like that, her crown had lit up and was twinkling like a brilliant tiny star!

Mr Not Right

"You want to hear something funny?" asked Max with a cheeky grin. We had just stopped to catch our breath after an energetic Cuban salsa routine.

"Sure," I replied.

"You know that guy you were dancing with before me? The one with the printed shirt over there?" he said, motioning to one end of the hall.

"You mean that one?" I confirmed, following his gaze.

"Yep, him," said Max.

"Funny you mention him – he just asked me out," I smirked.

"Aha! That makes sense. It's because he thinks you are someone else," said Max, grinning like the Cheshire Cat.

"Oh, *really*?" This had to be another one of his tall tales, I thought.

"Yes! You have a doppelganger who also comes here and he keeps chasing her around as well."

"You're joking!" I laughed. If it were true, then it was a rather funny story. "I've never seen any other girl here that looks like me."

"Yes! There is another Asian girl and she looks just like you!"

"No way!" I said, incredulous. "Well, in any case, I am not interested in him. He can go after Ms doppelganger. I much prefer his buddy," I said sheepishly, looking towards a dark-haired, Latin-looking guy, dancing just a short distance away.

"Who – *him*?" Max gave a look of mock disgust. "You really do pick 'em, don't ya?"

"Why? What's wrong with him?" I was beginning to regret my openness.

"He's a walking disaster. He just uses women. Don't waste your time."

I watched the couple dance, noticing the way Mr Latino overtly showed off his leading skills. "Hmm... well, maybe you're right. Maybe I should just give up, stop looking and go home. I'm so tired of having my heart broken," I sighed.

Max shrugged with a vague attempt at sympathy. Then, as is customary at salsa clubs, he sauntered off to find his next dance partner.

At the end of the evening, he approached me again to say goodbye.
"I was thinking," said Max, "about your problem".
"My problem?" Here we go again, I thought.
"There is another way, you know. To find the right person, that is. A friend of mine told me about it. All you have to do is just write it all down, everything you want in a man, like in real detail."
"Uh-huh… it's that simple?" I was amused but appreciated his desire to help. "What, do you mean like writing a list?"
"Yeah, kind of, but you have to be much more particular. You've got to write it and be really, really specific."
"And that works, does it? Have you tried it?"
"Err, well, uh… no, not yet. I will do if I ever think about settling down." He flashed his broad Cheshire grin again.
"Thanks, Max. I'll bear it in mind. See you next week," I said and we hugged each other goodbye.

For as long as I had known Max, he always seemed to enjoy the single life. His excuse was that he was too busy looking after the family business and caring for his parents to have time for girls. "Isn't it strange," I pondered, "how we kid ourselves with these kinds of 'cover-ups' and 'untruths' so that we can stay in our comfort zones. It keeps us from venturing into that unknown territory that might otherwise bring us the happiness we really want".

By now, my fairy tale dream of ever finding Mr Right had been quashed and crushed over and over again. It had gone through the wringer, was worn out and hanging on by just a few threads. After moving in with Pat, 'Mr totally wrong', and then moving out again after six months, it had become abundantly clear: my choices were getting steadily worse and the market for decent, available guys seemed thin on the ground. Of course, that was another untruth perpetuated by society and believed by many women in similar circumstances. It was an unfounded belief that I needed to change.

When I first introduced Pat to my friends and family, they had sniggered at his unconventional and weird way of being and made their pretentious opinions quite obvious. But I had long stopped caring about what others might think of me or who I was with. At first, all I saw was a genuinely jolly, happy chap who seemed delighted to be with me. Many months later, however, I discovered they were right: he was… well… completely nuts!

Pat, it turned out, was not only addicted to his hobby-cum-work in the entertainment business, but also to his need for smoking weed every day. Without it, he seemed unable to cope with normal life. If he could have kept things more balanced, perhaps I might have learned to live with it, but it over-shadowed his life and mine in many ways. Most of the time, he was also very self-absorbed and didn't know how to be a real friend or partner to me. Once again, I felt taken for granted, as though I was just something 'nice to have', like a pretty piece of furniture.

That year, my father passed away. Pat continued about his business as though nothing had happened and was unable to relate to me or my needs. He had no idea how to support or *be there* for me. It seemed that Pat was never going to change and I was feeling stuck. At the time, I was doing some freelance work for a company that slowly dissolved owing me several months pay and leaving me without any income. Unknowingly, I was slowly sinking into a depression and my usual enthusiasm for life was dwindling.

Eventually, I gathered my things and returned to my old home, feeling lost and let down. Pat had tried his best at the relationship but he was definitely not Mr Right. It was another bad choice that I'd made in haste when my heart was in a state of desperation. This was a tough lesson that I had to learn the hard way.

Life continued in limbo for a while and another year passed. I laid low, allowing myself to slowly return to some kind of normality and filled the emptiness with other distractions. "No more men! You must heal and repair your aching heart first," I told myself sternly. I forced myself not to think about relationships. Instead, I went out with friends, focused on doing the things I enjoyed and kept myself occupied by looking for work and keeping busy.

Luckily, within a matter of months, I managed to manifest exactly the job I had visualised, which turned out to be so much better than I had hoped for. The office was based only ten minutes' drive from home. I had plenty of autonomy with the scope for a promotion, possibilities for my own development and a great boss. The job was offered by an agency that had put me forward for a temporary position. However, after a lengthy and surprisingly 'wholesome' interview, my boss-to-be offered me a permanent post, saying that I had much more to offer than I gave myself credit. I was overjoyed because it gave me some much-needed stability and security. If only I could manifest the right man that easily.

Mr Fantastic

The princess had grown wiser, worldly and somewhat wider! But still, there was no sign of a suitable prince on the horizon. Now in her forties, the old dream of finding Mr Right resurfaced and rustled up her ruminations. "Isn't it time, yet? Or must I endure further trials?" she thought, feeling somewhat forlorn. "Dear Fairy Godmother – please, hear me. I really, really,

*really do not want any more lessons, **please**. Could you possibly, just find me **one** good one, perhaps even the right one?" she implored. "I promise to be more careful and discerning this time."*

Her fairy godmother wasn't amused and didn't answer. She had already told the princess to 'trust', meaning to have faith and be patient. Eventually, she felt a little sorry for the poor girl and simply said, "Don't go looking on the Internet again. Just write it down."

By that time, I had coached many clients on how to write their goals and helped them manifest what they really want. Then, I remembered Max's words and it occurred to me that I could write my wish list in the same way as I would write goals and positive affirmations. Interestingly, in the past, whenever I had written down something I wanted, it usually came into being without too much effort such as finding the right tenant or a handyman to fix my bathroom. "But, of course, those kind of things always work out for me because I am in control and can choose the person I want," I told myself. "When it comes to finding a man, a relationship, my wishes have no effect. I can't just pick one out of the Yellow Pages or website to do my biding! This is a matter of the heart so surely, I cannot have any influence over another human being's romantic feelings towards me. I can't *make that* happen." Obviously, this was yet another untruth that I had chosen to believe and which, needed to change.

I had also believed, as many do, that it was wrong to create such wish lists regarding Mr Right. Somehow, I felt it was too much of a tall order because I knew my endless wants and wishes were far too particular. "Shouldn't it be up to the gods to decide who is best for me?" I thought. Writing a detailed wish list seemed so very unromantic and unnatural, like planning and designing a new kitchen. Then again, isn't that exactly what I was doing every time I created my profile on a dating site? Perhaps the truth was, underneath it all, I was simply afraid of raising my hopes and having my expectations crushed again. Over the years, numerous wonderful things had appeared in my life through using the manifestation processes which I had cultivated, except for the one thing I longed for most.

It was the summer of 2008, and after receiving a few more whispers from the world, I concluded I would gain nothing if I didn't try. I sat down at my desk and decided it was time to put the long-held fantasy to paper. My imaginary, perfect Mr Right had remained locked up inside my dreams for long enough. "There's nothing to lose. I'll just do it for fun and not take it too seriously," I said to myself.

Before I began, as you might have guessed, I asked Fae for some guidance. Again, a steady stream of words flowed into my mind and poured out effortlessly, assimilating the myriad of needs, wants and desires together, which I had been mentally noting for years. Very soon, I had written a whole page describing how beautiful my loving, joyful relationship would be.

"This wonderful man is intelligent, consistent and considerate. He is sincere, calm and gentle but also able to deal with my fieriness when necessary. He understands and accepts me as I am; all my quirks, stubbornness, crazy notions and beliefs. Equally, I respect his needs, values, opinions and concerns. I appreciate and accept him just the way he is. The love I give him is truly deserved, for he is a good soul and it makes him feel wanted and needed" I wrote, allowing myself to feel the joy of already being with this man.

"He is a professional, such as an engineer, pilot, architect or academic and passionate about his work. He comes from a Latin or European background and we enjoy celebrating each other's cultural heritage. We are perfectly in tune and compatible. We are both completely committed to our relationship

and always supportive of each other. We see eye-to-eye most of the time, are the best of friends, laugh a lot together, etc, etc," I continued.

Interestingly, I thought of more characteristics I had never considered before that were also important to me, such as our relationships with each other's families. As I wrote, I tried not to think about how improbable my story was and that there was little likelihood of ever finding someone even halfway close to fulfilling it. When I had finished my fantastical story, I added a few pictures of loving couples, gave it a pretty border and printed it out. As I re-read it, a strange mixture of emotions washed over me; feelings of satisfaction, apprehension, and joy. I even felt tears of love and gratitude for this amazing man. "No more mistakes, okay? Now, I am totally sure I know what I want," I said to Fae as I slid my precious dream inside an envelope.
"Good. Now it is time to let go," said Fae. "Put it away and forget about it."

I tucked the envelope carefully inside a folder of old letters and memoirs, still feeling unsure about what I had just done. What if I had just jeopardised my chances by being too particular? How in the world was any man ever going to fit my incredibly specific criteria and such a complex combination of requirements? It was more than I could wish for, beyond any of my wildest dreams, that such a relationship could ever come true. "Well, don't worry," I reassured myself. "This is just a fantasy and as it is such a ludicrous wish list, it'll be easy to forget."

A few months later, I found myself going back and opening the dating website where Pat and I had met with the firm intention of deleting my account. "No harm in taking just one last look and then I will definitely close it down," but I was teasing myself. Before long, hours had passed and several profiles had caught my attention.

"Nice... hmm... but no, no, I'm really not interested," I said to myself, unconvincingly. My sensible brain was trying to dissuade me but failing, whilst my dragon was waiting in the wings, ready to pounce on the opportunity.

"Go on, just give it one more try," goaded Inge. "How else are you going to meet someone who actually suits you? At the salsa club? The supermarket? Any of the guys at work? Don't be silly! You'll never meet someone by going to the same places, doing the same old thing and just waiting. You know you haven't got all the time in the world," it hissed into my ear. "And anyway, you're so picky. The Internet is the best place to go. You have all the choice in the world there and can be really selective."

It was too tempting. "Well, at least this website is for more mature, discerning individuals," I rationalised and let myself be persuaded. "Only if there happens to be one or two genuinely worthy candidates and they are a hundred per cent the kind of guy I want." I simply couldn't go through another break-up. My heart wouldn't cope. "This time, for sure, I *will* find Mr Right, the one I am meant to be with."

Very soon, I was messaging an enigmatic stranger who seemed to match many of my criteria. It was uncanny how well we were getting along with just the first few messages to each other. After our first telephone call, I felt this had to be the one. He seemed to fit perfectly! "Surely, the gods have answered my wishes this time and my prince has at last arrived," I thought, feeling elated. The chemistry, conversation and his natural charisma held me in an enchanted spell. There were no negative gut feelings or early warning signs on our first date, probably because I was too wrapped up in my own excited, love bubble and didn't notice that I was meandering down a rocky road, set on a course to self-implode.

It didn't take long for the full picture to emerge. Alas, my Mr Perfect story was just that; a fantasy story. The relationship with Rick turned out to be the exact opposite of everything that I had written about. This rollercoaster ride was much harder than anyone or anything I had ever encountered. Many of my previous bad experiences had all combined together and reappeared in this one horrible nightmare relationship.

When it was over, I tried desperately to fathom where I stood in my journey of love lessons but nothing made sense. "What in the world am I supposed to learn from all this? Haven't I been given enough lessons already? How on earth did I end up here? And why, oh why, does it hurt *so much?*" My mind was in turmoil as I began to think that perhaps, the gods were trying to punish me or something for not listening to Fae's advice.

"What if I really am stupid because I just don't understand what I'm supposed to understand? Perhaps I was never cut out for relationships, having children or marriage after all. I've just been fooling myself all this time and I am actually supposed to live my life alone," I thought, feeling utterly despondent, hurt and furious with myself for getting into yet another mess. I had absolutely no clue what or how to heal or move forward. My brain was in a whirl and could not compute any logical answers.

Indeed, I had reached the end of my tolerance level and my heart was smashed to pieces. I was teetering on the brink of no return. After experiencing the wrath of Rick, I withdrew from life and cocooned myself in inside my personal cave. Apart from work and the supermarket, I went into hermit mode and avoided friends, family and going out. I had never expected that my life could take such a turn but at the time, my mind, body and soul were crying out for solitude and comfort. Those months of grief, mourning over my past, were exactly what I needed.

What I wasn't yet aware of was that the gods had already made other plans for me...

Trove of Treasures

The road ahead was blurry and my fog lights were not working. Without a doubt, this route was not one I would ever have chosen to drive along. I stumbled along that long, miserable journey through the dark tunnel, clutching onto my one solace; meditation and confiding in my dear Fae. She advised me to blindly trust whatever may come. Thankfully, she did not once reprimand me for ignoring her advice about not Internet dating again. On the contrary, she wrapped me in swathes of kindness and compassion, reassuring me that all would be taken care of. Through it all, despite the agony, pain and my confidence being knocked, my core beliefs held strong and I had an unwavering faith knowing that, at some point, this storm too, shall pass.

During the following year, I received the precise guidance I needed to help me clear my basement of all the unwanted baggage which I had accumulated over several decades. Certainly, this custom-made programme of learning, designed specifically for my deepest healing, could never have been devised or conducted by a psychotherapist, coach or any other mind specialist. No other human being could have known *me* as well as my Fae.

To give you an idea, here are some of the lessons I learnt:

- How to navigate and release through the grieving process gradually, day by day.
- How to recognise and tame my dragon; face my fears and replace negative patterns.

- Learning how to and whom I should forgive.
- How to stop worrying and learning to TRUST the process of my healing journey.
- Learning the various methods of how to increase my self-worth.
- Being shown exactly how to accept that 'I deserve to be totally happy'.
- Learning what true gratitude can do to change my energy.

Through the course of this book, I have shared most of my lessons with you but of course, one size does not fit all. Only your soul will know exactly what and how best to provide the right lessons for you. Therefore, if you wish to re-examine, learn and heal from your past, I urge you to listen to your own inner guidance, as your lessons will be uniquely relevant to your circumstances, specific needs and individual growth.

The months rolled by as I uncorked all the unhealthy emotions that had been bottled away for decades and slowly letting them drain out of my system. As I emptied myself of those negative beliefs, painful memories, guilt and grievances, I found my heart no longer feeling empty, nor did it hunger for love as it had done before. That space naturally began to fill up with an abundance of self-love, compassion and acceptance. Now, this was a novel and joyous feeling which I had never felt before and certainly, not for myself. It was the kind of love that one might have for his/her newborn child or a beloved pet. This is a very natural, pure love that exudes from deep within your soul and does not need a reason other than it simply is.

At that juncture in my life, this psychological cleansing was the most appropriate course of healing that I could ever hoped to have. Many years later, when I looked back on the chain of events and the relationships leading up to that point, I was able to appreciate the stages I went through and their perfect synchronicity. I understood just how necessary each and every encounter, challenge and heartbreak was in my healing journey.

One very significant lesson was learning that the people you attract are all, in some way, reflections of yourself. This helped me understand why I had to experience those last couple of tough relationships, just when I thought I was done with lessons. It was in order to take the final leap and go inside to focus on healing myself mentally and emotionally.

After writing my story about my perfect future partner, the wheels had been set in motion to align my compass to my true north. Meeting Rick at that particular point in my life was no coincidence. It was the catalyst that catapulted me out of a redundant old mindset and forced me, not only to 'clean my plates', but de-clutter my entire kitchen!

This extraordinary awakening made the princess realise she didn't need to travel across the world or find her prince because **she always had the power** *inside herself. All she needed to do was to click her heels and learn to use that power; the magic of her thoughts. Then, take a deep look into her own eyes in the mirror and shed the last few heavy bags which no longer served her. At last, she found the deepest joy and peace, knowing she was, indeed, worthy, loveable and imperfectly perfect, just as she was. The fairy godmother smiled, satisfied with her achievement and urged the princess to put her crown back on, for it was time that the true, authentic princess to emerge.*

But before I go on with my story, it is time for you to write yours. Now, it is your turn to cast a magic spell to attract the person of your dreams into your life. Thank you for having waited patiently and trusting me with all the steps thus far. Actually, not me, but trusting yourself and doing all the challenging inner work; well done!

All you need now is to remember a few special ingredients for preparing this powerful potion: It takes a packet of patience, a handful of trust and a bunch of intrinsic belief, carefully mixed together inside a heart full of love.

I recommend that you keep an open mind whilst doing the following exercises. It is best to not divulge all to your friends but to keep these methods to yourself. Why? Because your magic beans need to take root in the fertile ground of your beautiful vision and should not be soiled by other's doubts. All you need to do is to plant and nurture them, then rest awhile. Eventually, once your garden is in full bloom, you will be able to share your marvellous trove of treasures with those who really want to know.

LESSON 8: Making Magic

In order to create an authentic brew, you must first wash your utensils, sterilise pots and clear the workspace. In other words, if you have done the tasks and followed the steps given in each of the chapters so far, you will have completed the necessary work to dig out and release past baggage from your subconscious mind. If you haven't, you will most likely attract another relationship that recreates the same problems and patterns as you had before. Therefore, it is very important to create a healthy space in your heart and mind before you embark on making magic spells to attract the right kind of love into your life.

Now, that you are ready, let's take the next step into the kingdom of happy-ever-after and manifest your true Mr or Ms Right! I know you are excited but try not to put too much pressure on yourself or worry if you are doing it exactly right. Again, in the following meditation you may feel like you are making it all up which is absolutely fine. Simply *allow* your creative mind to lead, go with the flow and enjoy the experience.

A. Visualising Your Ideal Partner

As you are already fairly well-practised with these visualising meditation exercises, you should be able to get your body and mind into a relaxed state easily. Again, choose a time and place where you will be undisturbed so you can be calm and concentrate. You will only need to do this meditation once but make sure you do it wholeheartedly.

As usual, I recommend you record these instructions into a voice recorder, then settle down and simply listen to it using earphones. You may also like to light a candle and play some tranquil background meditation music to help you relax.

1. As before, get into a comfortable position and ready to relax. Close your eyes.
2. Take three long, deep breaths, letting go of all thoughts from the day. Put to one side any anxieties or concerns about this meditation or anything else that may be on your mind.
3. Count backwards from 10 to 1 in your mind and with each number, feel your body becoming more and more relaxed. Focus on different parts of your body and release any tension. Take your time to relax your whole body.
4. Breathe normally and allow your mind to unwind as you go down into a deep, relaxed state. Imagine you are now walking outside along a path in your favourite peaceful place. You feel very calm here and this is exactly where you want to be right now.
5. Take in the scenery and sounds and smells of everything around you. Enjoy this beautiful day and the calmness of nature.
6. Now, head to your garden. Go through the gate and enter the house as you did before. You are now in your special room where you can create magic. You feel positive, relaxed and centred. It is good to be here again. If you wish, you can invite your IGS to join you.
7. Take a seat on your comfy sofa and pick up the remote control. Switch on your screen. Press the number buttons for a year that is a few years ahead from now. See the year appear on your screen.
8. Press 'play'. Immediately, a video starts to play, showing a very happy future scene of you at home. You are feeling very calm, content and happy with your life.
9. The front door opens and your new life partner walks in and greets you warmly. You know this is your ideal partner, best friend and soul mate. You are both very, very happy together and you suit each other perfectly. It feels so right, easy and comfortable being with him/her.

10. Imagine doing some everyday activity together such as preparing dinner or relaxing in the living room. Notice your partner's behaviours and actions as you enjoy each other's company. Become aware of his/her personality, expression and behaviour. Allow your mind to dwell on how you good the feeling is just being with her/him. Notice how he/she feels about you.
11. Now, in your mind, say this statement and add the words that feel natural for you: I am so grateful and happy to be with this man/woman. He/she deserves me because I am... And I deserve him/her because...
12. Imagine taking the person's hands in yours and *feel* the feeling of being deeply connected, accepted and loved just as you are. You know that you both want and appreciate each other completely. This person is everything you ever imagined and your dream has come true. Feel extremely satisfied, glad and grateful for having this loving human being in your life. Tell her/him how grateful you are. Enjoy these emotions.
13. Now, imagine taking a snapshot of this perfect image. Wrap it in love and positive light and hang it on your wall in your special room.
14. Turn off the screen and let go of all that you have seen.
15. Take a deep breath and release the experience. Come back to wakefulness as usual by returning the way you came in. Take your time to count yourself back slowly from 1 to 10 and become more awake with each number.
16. When you are ready, open your eyes, feeling refreshed and at peace.

When you have finished the meditation, write down in your notebook all the details you perceived of your life partner, and anything else you noticed, whilst viewing the future. Do not question or try to analyse anything with your awake, logical mind just yet. Before going on to

B, the next writing exercise, take at least a day's break after doing this meditation

Once you have completed the full meditation, I recommend that you imagine only the final part regularly for about a month or two afterwards. Simply think about the happy snapshot and enjoy the feeling of being together. Do not allow any negative thoughts to cloud your perfect image. Do this as a short visualisation when you are relaxed or meditating. Usually, after you wake up in the morning and/or at night before sleep is best. This will embed the positive image into your subconscious mind.

B. Your Ideal Relationship Story

For this exercise, you must cast aside any preconceived ideas or expectations about relationships that are not genuinely your own. Also, do not think of this as writing a 'wish list'. Instead, think of it as writing a creative, beautiful, idealistic dream story and put aside any logical reasoning.

You can start by writing this directly in your paper notebook or on a computer but I suggest that your final copy is handwritten and on paper.

1. Take a long, deep breath and say to yourself, "I am now designing my perfect future and the right words are coming to me easily".
2. On a fresh page, write a title such as, 'Me and My Perfect Life-Partner'.
3. Bring to mind the person you visualised in exercise A: your ideal partner. Again, imagine you are already in this relationship and you are both completely happy together.

4. Write a description of the relationship and your partner. Start by doing a 'brain dump' of all the words and relevant points that come to mind. You can also refer to the Know Thyself exercise in Chapter Five for descriptive words. You can include points such as the following in your story:

a) About your ideal partner:
- Character and personality
- Core beliefs/values and how these coincide with yours
- Background, education level, work ethic, etc.
- Family status and family values
- Age, figure, external looks (if important to you)
- How he/she feels about you
- What she/he likes about you
- What you give that makes him/her happy

b) About yourself:
- How you feel for her/him
- How you behave and act with him/her
- How you feel supported to grow/learn/be yourself
- Why it feels so good
- What he/she gives you that makes you happy

c) About your relationship together:
- Living arrangements
- Level of communication and humour
- How you interact together
- About your goals, beliefs, trust, reliability, etc.
- How you interact with each other's friends and family

- How you feel for each other when apart
- Why he/she deserves you and you deserve her/him

5. Then, put these words into sentences. Start your story with a sentence, such as, "Today, I am so grateful and happy because I have met (and married/settled down with) my ideal soul partner."
6. Write it using positive, affirmative words and not negative ones (e.g., instead of saying, "She is not too loud and talkative," you can say, "She is rather quiet and thoughtful").
7. The most important element is to write your story as though it has *already happened* by using the present or past tenses (e.g., do not write in future tense such as, "He will be a caring person," but instead write, "He is a caring person").
8. End your story with how grateful you are for this incredible relationship.
9. Once you have finished, read through and correct it. Leave it for a day or two and then, add or amend anything you feel necessary. Ensure you are completely satisfied that it includes all of the elements that are most important to you in a relationship.
10. Finally, put away the notes of your ideal relationship story in a place where you will no longer look at it. Release it from your conscious mind and do not dwell on it again. If you wish, you can ask your IGS to take over and say that you now leave this in his or her capable hands. It is time to allow your subconscious mind, life and the forces of nature to do their work.

Note: I have used the words, 'perfect' and 'ideal' synonymously to describe the best kind of partner or relationship for you. This means a partner who fits your needs and you fit theirs perfectly, which includes all of your imperfections and those of your partner. To avoid misinterpretation, this does not mean the person is absolutely perfect or the relationship is 100% ideal. We are all human which means that absolute perfection is impossible and should never be expected. We are, therefore, striving towards having an 'ideal relationship', which means that both of you are feeling good, healthy and happy together for the majority of the time.

C. Reality versus Imagination

Now, you are probably wondering how this manifestation magic actually works. Perhaps you are a little dubious, especially since the above exercises seem so simple. I understand. When I first wrote my happy-ever-after story, I too, did not believe it would make any difference. Moreover, I had been visualising my ideal partner for many years but it had never worked out particularly well. It was only after years of practice that I finally learned the right formula for manifestation.

You see, it has a lot to do with what happens inside our amazing brains. According to the latest scientific research, there are several psychological factors that contribute to this process which are worth noting. Firstly, our conscious brain deals with the thoughts that we are normally aware of. It is where most of our problem solving, logical and practical thinking processes take place. However, it is only responsible for less than 10% of the activity that actually takes place in our brains. The other 90% or more is managed by our very powerful subconscious brain.[17]

We are designed to be unaware of much of the activity taking place in our subconscious brain because Mother Nature, in her infinite wisdom, has ensured that we do not have to cope with the huge amount of data processing and decision making that needs to be done at any given moment. Certainly, if we were aware, we would probably make a mess of it and probably, forget to breathe or close our eyes when dust flies at us.

Most of the hard-wiring in your brain is in your subconscious, which is where your default programmes are also installed, and these have been running since you came into existence. It also manages the huge number of automatic physiological and psychological functions that are constantly working yet do not need our conscious attention. Therefore, the subconscious filters through all the data and decides which bits to allow into our conscious brain that we might need to pay attention to. This is done by the 'Reticular Activating System', which is a particular network of neurons housed in the brain stem.[18] Apart from being responsible for various other functions, it provides this filtering activity by mediating our behaviours and bringing conscious awareness to those things we think about more often.

Therefore, the more you bring a particular thing into focus and dwell upon it, the more you notice it, and the less likely you are to miss an opportunity. As your brain becomes 'habituated' to recognising a specific thing, this filter system functions more efficiently and automatically attracts your attention to that which you have been focusing on. Hence, we *perceive* more of whatever we choose to experience; whether it is sickness, strife or stressful relationships or, on the contrary, joyful, healthy and abundant experiences. When you relax your mind and meditate, you can access this part of your brain and re-programme it to focus on the things you really want.

This brain process is also dependent on our beliefs and can manifest all manner of things. It does so by recreating anything we feed those beliefs with. In other words, if we spend our time imagining the world is against us, life is a struggle, or that all men/women are difficult, that is precisely what we will see, hear and feel more often. On the other hand, when we believe that life is good and plentiful and trust in receiving the best from others, then we will experience exactly that.

Secondly, despite the extraordinary abilities of our subconscious mind, it is not very good at differentiating between that which is an actual experience and one that is imagined.[19] For instance, we might perceive a situation to be traumatic, whether it actually was or not, and thereafter, it may continue to cause terrible harm mentally and emotionally for years to come. By replaying that event in our minds, it will have the same nasty psychological and physical effects as it did initially, even though the actual event only happened once many years ago.

Similarly, we can create an imagined positive experience devoid of any bad influence, and our subconscious brain will react to it as if it were real. When our subconscious brain has seen, felt and heard that experience with all of its (imagined) senses, it will believe that it was an actual event and act as though it has already happened. Hence, you will start to attract those kinds of experiences and *coincidences* into your life that align with whatever your subconscious mind has been focusing on.

Now, let's suppose that the above Making Magic Exercises are simply about getting your mind to focus and be totally clear and precise about what you actually desire instead of focusing on what you *do not* want. If we are unaware of our negative thought programmes and beliefs, our filter system will ensure that the subconscious mind continues to recreate the negative experiences of the past. Hence, it can easily taint our future choices, distract our focus and bring us more of what we don't want, such as further heartbreak. This is why I have dedicated so much of this book to help you remove those unconscious barriers and burdens that have caused you heartache in the past.

If you were to buy a house, a new car or find a new job, you would not leave it to chance or fate, would you? After all, you don't want to take unnecessary risks with such important things that are very expensive, valuable or life changing. You would, of course, do your homework, make a list of your requirements, assess finances, check the particulars and decide beforehand what, when and how things should be done to suit your individual needs. Once you have established a clear idea and plan, you would take the necessary actions based on informed, well-calculated judgement. Hence, you would try to steer the respective elements as best you could, and which are within your control, to bring you the outcomes you desire.

In the same way, let's presume that your ideal life-partner already exists somewhere out there on this planet and that he or she is also looking for someone just like you. All you need to do is to get her or his trajectory to cross your own. Therefore, the exercises I have given work on aligning your subconscious with that of your future partner by eliminating all the unnecessary clutter and bringing your mind's attention sharply into focus. Your unconscious antenna will now tune into the necessary frequencies that will help you take the right actions and move naturally toward making your dream a reality. In the next chapter, I give further explanations about how the mind affects the manifestation process.

Ticket to the Ball

The bleakness that had once engulfed the castle slowly cleared as the princess began to wake from a long slumber filled with nightmares. As the sun began to stream in once more, she felt as though she had been away for years and forgotten who she once was. Stepping outside into the garden, she took a deep breath of cool, fresh air and let the last of her heavy clouds melt away. Very soon, she was feeling like her old self again. The jovial, gentle princess, her most natural self, was now returning and she happily cooked up a delicious meal to restore her energy. It was good to be alive, to have her own castle and purposeful work. Little did she know that life was yet again, about to change dramatically and take on a whole new perspective.

After months of darkness and having done all that Fae had instructed me to do, I finally began to see a speck of light at the end of the tunnel. The overwhelming sorrow and sadness started to recede and I felt something shift inside me. As the tears began to dry up, I wondered if this really was the end or just a short respite before it began again.

"What's happening? Is it really over? Or is there going to be another wave?" I asked. Perhaps, I was just seeing a mirage in the desert, created by my own desperate thirst.
Fae smiled gently and said, "My dear, you have been through enough".
"Yes, but I just don't know if it's really over yet," I said, doubting myself. "I don't want to go through that old routine of pulling myself up by my own bootstraps again and ignoring my true emotions. I never want to go back to being that way."
"You don't need to cry anymore, my dear," she said, and I felt her warmth wrap around me. "Are you still feeling hurt?"
"No, actually, not as much as I did before," I replied. It was true. At last, those depressed feelings had diminished.
"Then, trust what you are feeling."

"What should I do now?" I felt a little anxiety creeping in.
Her answer was immediate, "It's time to re-join the world and come out of hiding. But remember: be kind to yourself".

I felt strangely apprehensive as I started to contact my old friends and family again. Could I really go out and start enjoying life again? This was something I had grown unused to. It felt like being a nervous teenager all over again, worried about going to my first grown-up party.

Fae had advised that I should be kind to myself which meant taking small steps. I started by slowly going back to having a little social life and seeing just one or two friend at the weekends. It was still too soon for me to open up and talk about all that I had gone through but at least I could smile and enjoy their warm welcome.

The months rolled rapidly by and it was almost December. I found myself enjoying going to my favourite salsa club again, making new friends and being invited to Christmas parties. As always, there were one or two men there who seemed rather keen. "Why is it that when I am not at all interested, I have guys chasing me, and when I am looking, there's no one to be found?" I was reflecting on the previous evening when I had met, not one, but three nice bachelor friends. Fae had just smiled and said, "Not them". All I kept seeing was the word 'trust' in big letters emblazoned across my screen whenever I asked about my future.

Anyway, this was certainly not the time to be meeting someone new — not at all! This was *my time* to regain balance, take care of number one and get myself together. I was still in the process of healing and recovering. All I wanted was to breathe and feel my feet on the ground again. However, it seemed that even Fae was trying to set me up. A day or two later, she greeted me with great enthusiasm. "Hello, hello! Come in," she said. I had barely closed my eyes and entered my special room. "There is someone we want you to meet. Look!"

I looked towards the space that she was indicating, and in the distance, I saw there was the figure of a man. Although it was just a shadowy figure, and I could not make out any features, I knew at once what her intention was.

"Oh, goodness, no... please, no! I really, *really* do not want to meet anyone right now." I said, feeling a little disappointed with Fae. "I just can't handle that; not now, thank you." I know I was a bit short with her but honestly, this was quite exasperating. How could she – whom I most relied upon – think that meeting a man at this point in my life would be a good idea?

I was done with being hurt and refused to go through the hell of heartbreak yet again. I was done with all the crying, releasing and forgiving. I had had quite enough of trying to make relationships work and working so hard on healing myself. Self-work is hard work and I needed a break, a proper break. I just wanted to be alone for a while and get back to being happy within myself again, without a man!

After what seemed like an age, I was at last feeling good about life again and content in my own skin. The authentic me had finally arrived and I wasn't going to take any steps backwards. Now, there was no more need for false pretences or desperation, and I had absolutely no hunger to be with anyone. My life was just beginning to take off again and it was time to just be happy with all that I had. Every day, I felt incredibly grateful for all the small things: good food in my belly, nice colleagues, my reliable car, etc. And of course, I was especially thankful for the important things: my stable job, beloved home, reliable tenants, the gifts of friendship and an adoring cat – what more could I need?

It was good to put on a pretty dress again to go to the Christmas parties but soon, the holidays were over, and I was back at work in full swing. One frosty morning in early January, my boss called me into his office. "As you know, we have been discussing how to manage the financial crisis," he began and then, went on to explain the current situation with cutbacks, etc. "So er... the directors have decided that they will have to make at least 30% of the staff redundant... unfortunately." He hesitated, obviously feeling uncomfortable and scratched his head. "Uh... I wish there was another way but... Well, I am so sorry but we have to let you go, too." He said, looking clearly uncomfortable. He was feeling terrible about having to have this conversation with one of his best members of staff.

As you can imagine, I was shocked and it took several moments for me to take it all in. "Oh, okay... my goodness – I did not see that coming," was all I could say.

My mind began to whirl, "Wow! Am I really losing my job? Is this really happening to me?" I thought to myself. "And just when I was planning some great new projects for this year. Well... I guess the good thing is that I didn't do anything wrong," I consoled myself.

"You'll be fine, don't worry," Fae whispered from the back of my head. "You can temp for a while like you've always done."

"How on earth will you manage without me? Who's going to laugh at all your terrible jokes?" I said to my boss, with a half-hearted grin, trying to lighten the load. My boss also gave an unconvincing smile and explained that, unfortunately, it was a case of 'last in, first out'.
"You know the problem is, as you've done so well at implementing the new self-development systems and training programmes... well, you've pretty much done yourself out of a job," he explained. I didn't feel the

same because I knew there was still a lot more work to do. My current projects were far from complete but I chose not to argue with him.

We went on to discuss my redundancy package, as well as a strategy for sharing out my tasks and responsibilities with the other team managers because of course, they would not be taking on anyone else to replace me. My poor boss was feeling somewhat guilty and he kindly offered to support me by writing a glowing reference and updating my CV himself.

At the end of our discussion, I stood up and shook his hand. "Thank you for all the opportunities and always supporting me. I don't know what's around the corner for me but anyway, I am grateful to you for letting me go. I have a good feeling," I said, smiling sadly.
"Without a doubt," he agreed, looking a little surprised. No one had ever thanked him for being made redundant before.

As I cleared out my desk, I felt a mixture of sadness and anxiety. After all, it was the best job I'd ever had. Yet, at the same time, I felt a calmness and certainty deep within me, as though I knew there was a good reason for it all. One of the great many lessons I have received in life is that there is little point in getting overwrought about situations over which I have absolutely no control. It was better to take stock and focus my energy on moving forward.

For me, it was better to resign myself to the situation and simply have gratitude for whatever lay ahead. Within a few days, I had digested the facts, re-evaluated my situation and made a new plan for finding work. First of all, I would go back to the employment agencies and find some temporary work. Then, I would take a short holiday, and after that, I would start job hunting in earnest.

Normally, I would have taken my vacation around Easter time but now it didn't make sense to have a holiday already booked and start a possible new job. It would be better to take a break sooner to recharge my batteries. After all, I had earned it. The past year had probably been one of the hardest I'd ever had, and as I'm sure you've guessed, Fae guided me through every step of the way. However, she had omitted one little fact, or perhaps, I didn't notice the hints. Behind the scenes, she was cooking up a plot that, by hook or by crook, Cinderella needed to go to the ball. She would make sure that the princess must get her ticket even if that meant losing her job.

I checked my budget and then, happily gazed at a world map on the Internet. "So, where have I not yet been that I can go now and can afford?" I pondered. It was always exciting for me to explore somewhere new. After searching through various holidays, prices and packages, I found three possible options: Tunisia, Egypt or the Canaries. All offered some winter sunshine and a little interesting sightseeing. Well, Egypt would be great and it had been on my list for years as I'd always wanted to see the pyramids. Also, Tunisia sounded fascinating but being a lone traveller, well, I wasn't quite sure…

"Hmm… now this looks interesting," I thought, as I spotted a travel site saying that there might be a carnival in the Canaries next month. "Follow your heart," urged Fae.

Well, I suppose it was about time to enjoy the things I loved most again. "Oh, I don't know – it might be rubbish, and I have already been to Spain and the Balearic Islands before," I mulled, trying to decide. "But then again, I do love all things Spanish, especially the music." Inevitably, the promise of Latin vibes and salsa dancing was more enticing, and very soon, I had booked my flights and hotel for a week on one of the Canary Islands.

It was a cold, grey February day in England when I happily boarded the plane, took my window seat and settled down for the four-and-a-half-hour flight. "This is going to be *my* holiday, *my* time, just for *me*," I affirmed to myself. "No great expectations. And no matter what the place is like, I'm going make the best of it." Once again, I was back in my comfort zone, travelling alone and loving every minute of it. The familiar, old 'travel bug' feeling of anticipation bubbled in my belly. Some warm sunshine and time to rest, ruminate and realign. This was exactly what my soul needed.

Other than looking forward to the holiday, I was already feeling much happier and complete within myself. I had begun to have a much greater sense of being centred, more than I had ever felt before, despite losing my job and only temping. It felt so liberating, knowing that I had at last thrown out the old desperation, doubts and default programmes. Gone was the need to affect a smile or please others all the time. Those layers had been shed along with all the unnecessary excess baggage. I found myself feeling lighter and freer in my interactions than ever, less concerned about doing what was right or expected, and more able to be the *who* I am. It was an amazing feeling of, not just being me, but a more whole, healthier and authentic version of me that I hadn't known before.

10. An Enchanted Island

'Twas the night of the Great Enchantment Ball and all the creatures had gathered at the pond. The fireflies flickered as the music called her towards the centre. Settling on a lily pad, she swayed happily, marveling at the wondrous creatures making merry.

Then suddenly, a joyful stranger appeared at her side. "You dance so gracefully, my lady," he said. "May I have the pleasure?"
"Oh, my," she answered, pleasantly surprised. "You wish to dance... with **me**?"
"Why yes, I would be delighted," he beamed and held out his hand. She hesitated for only a moment before diving into the water with him.

And so, they danced and danced. They danced to the Frogstrot and the Cinderella Swirl and before she knew it, hours had passed by. Till at last, weary but joyful, they stopped to rest awhile.

"Isn't it curious that we have not met before?" she said. "Yet dancing with you is as easy as stepping into old shoes".
He scratched his head and nodded.
"Well, I am certain you must be a prince," she went on, "or at least a knight? For you, too, dance most elegantly."
"Oh, thank you." he replied, blushing. "Ah no, I'm afraid not. I am but a mere frog. Why, indeed, **you** must be a princess."
"You are most gallant. Thank you," she replied. "Perhaps, I am... but it matters not, for I am all that you see in my eyes."

Dancing Feet

The atmosphere buzzed with the energy of jubilant carnival revellers. There were people of every generation and background lining the streets, wearing colourful costumes and bright smiles. The stallholders were happily selling snacks, drinks and novelties whilst music coursed from every angle. Despite their copious drinking, there was never a hint of unfriendly or nasty behaviour. "The Spanish certainly know how to have fun," I thought and laughed at the antics of another group of guys dressed in outlandish, homemade costumes, teasing the crowds as they came staggering past.

It was the night of the hilarious 'Men in High Heels Race', a spectacular and comical event that had little to do with racing or competition. This was a parade with the only prerequisite being that the participants had to be men wearing ridiculously high heels! Groups of, otherwise ordinary men, dressed up in outrageous costumes or women's clothes, tottered along the promenade and down some cobbled streets whilst becoming increasingly inebriated and entertaining the crowds. Eventually, they reached the finish line at the town square where a winner was announced and the merriment continued for the rest of the night. "I had no idea that 'carnival' meant this much fun." I mused, watching their antics and clicking away with my camera.

The sheer size and extent of the festivities taking place were quite astounding and I must have worn a permanent grin on my face since I arrived. There had also been some kind of celebration the evening before, involving one float that looked like a huge fish with processions of people dressed in mourning clothes following behind it. Although, they didn't seem at all mournful and joyfully made their way along the same cobbled street route down to the marina. From where I stood at the back, there was not much to see except for the huge bonfire at the water's edge, followed by a fantastic fireworks show. Later, a band started setting up to play on the stage in the main square, although it was already eleven-thirty at night!

After a year of being locked away in her castle, the princess was so grateful and excited to have arrived at such a fantastic place full of festive people having fun. Here, at last, she could say goodbye to the heartaches of yesterday and embrace her authentic self, the true treasure, which she had finally found. It was time to celebrate the return of her joyful self and seize the spirit of the carnival, but tonight, she was very tired and the merriment would have to wait till the next day.

Meanwhile, unbeknownst to the princess, her fairy godmother had been conjuring up a powerful potion of enchantment to ensure that even if Cinderella missed this one, she would definitely go to the next ball and dance till dawn.

Despite being exhausted after a long day of travelling, I could hardly sleep on my first night there as the music continued to blare until at least five in the morning. My hotel was less than half a mile from the square and it was only after an early breakfast that I could get some sleep. Later that afternoon, I enjoyed wandering around the little town, getting my bearings and taking a revitalising walk along the seafront and marina.

Being near the sea always soothed my soul and renewed my senses. My heart was feeling whole again. I felt content to simply take in the new sites, sit at a café and enjoy my favourite pastimes; reading a book and watching people. This was the peace I had wished for. The town felt strangely comfortable, as though I belonged there and had come home. There was nothing to hamper my blissful enjoyment of just *being*.

Now, it was past midnight and once again, the band started booming out Latin music in the square as the crazy Men's High Heel Race came to an end. I had made sure to take a *siesta* that afternoon and recharge my batteries because no doubt, it would be another long night of frivolity, fun and festivities. "If I had known, I would have brought a fancy-dress outfit," I thought, marvelling at some of the costumes passing by. But my ordinary, casual clothes really didn't matter as no one cared how I looked. I sensed no pretension or judgement by the people. They were there to simply have fun and enjoy themselves.

I found myself in a bar near the marina with some older British guys who were dressed in outrageous drag outfits! They seemed to be having a hilarious time and warmly invited me to join them. I stayed for one drink and then wandered back outside as the live music was calling me. Needless to say, the Latin beats were pumping out from the energetic band on stage whilst people sang along and danced in the square.

I meandered my way through the throng, swaying happily, letting the rhythm vibrate through me. The music called for a 'merengue'; a simple, two-step, fast paced dance which most of the people seemed to be doing without the need of a partner. The pulsating tempo was energising and it absorbed my whole being. As I drank in the atmosphere and stepped to the beat, I felt completely in my element.

Then, the band started rolling out some salsa songs and my feet automatically switched to the three/seven-step dance. "Oh, yeah! Now, all I need is a partner," I thought and looked around for someone to dance with. One jolly young man stepped confidently towards me, taking my hand. "Do you salsa?" I asked but he couldn't hear or understand me over the noise. He simply grinned and continued attempting to follow my steps. After a few ungainly twists and twirls, it was clear he didn't know how. "Sorry... no... thank you," I said, smiling and pulling back. He didn't seem to mind and continued dancing by himself when I moved on.

Then, another rather tall, cheerful chap repeated the same routine. Again, I moved away mouthing a sorry and continued weaving my way through the exuberant dancers. "How strange; it seems most of the Spanish people here don't seem to know how to dance salsa." Then, just as I was about to give up my search, across the crowds, I spotted two feet moving to, what seemed like, salsa steps. "Aha! Is that what I think it is?" I moved a little closer to look. "Yes, it is!" I thought, grinning to myself and wound my way towards those feet, searching to find who might be attached to them.

My eyes followed the dancing feet that led to the legs, up the body and came to rest on a happy face. His eyes were half-closed, consumed by the music as he moved to a salsa side to side step. I was in front of him now, mirroring his steps. As his eyes fell upon me, I held out my hands and he seemed pleasantly surprised. I didn't need to speak. He only hesitated for a moment before stepping forward and taking me into a gentle partner hold.

We stepped into a familiar Cuban routine, dancing easily together but the song ended too soon and we had to stop. Immediately, the next salsa tune started and he asked me if I wanted another dance. Of course, I nodded enthusiastically, as he was a very good lead. It seemed we were both equally delighted to enjoy a partner's dance and we merged into the music once more.

Alas, the next song ended and we politely thanked each other and I went on my way, disappearing into the crowd again. That was enough for now. It was time to take a little break. I walked around the square, got myself a cool lemonade and stood beside the drinks stand where I could watch the band. "It is so fantastic being here! I can dance, have fun and meet equally carefree people. It's exactly what my soul needed," I thought. "I must remember to thank Fae later. This holiday was definitely the right choice and the perfect treat to give myself after all the hardships of last year. I deserve this." I stood, soaking up the atmosphere, wiggling to the music and watching the jubilant people around me.

"That was such a lovely dance with Mr Happy Face. It's not often I get to dance with someone who is that easy and comfortable to dance with," I thought, sipping my drink, "and how lucky to find someone who can salsa so well amongst so many people who don't. He also seemed like a really nice guy, quite courteous and not pushy at all. Hmm, I wonder where he might be." I craned my neck, looking towards the spot where we had danced, searching for a bald head amongst the crowd. "It might be nice to have another dance later on," I hoped but it was too dark to make out the faces in the constantly moving mass of people.

"Ah well, if he was actually interested in dancing with me again, he would have asked. He's probably busy dancing with someone else now. Never mind. Forget it," I concluded and reminded myself of why I had come on holiday. "Now, behave. It was just a nice dance – that was all. You're not looking for anything else, remember? You're here to just have fun *on your own*."

As I was engrossed in my own thoughts, I suddenly felt a light tap on my shoulder. "Excuse me. Hello." As if by magic, or perhaps he'd read my mind, I turned to find Mr Happy Face standing beside me.
"Oh, hello again," I said, pleasantly surprised. We introduced ourselves to each other. His name was Pete and he was there with his friend, Ben, and they were both from Germany. He too, was on holiday and so, we chatted easily about the carnival.

When he discovered I was alone, he said, "Oh, you don't have to be alone. Come join us, if you like?"

"Well... eh... thank you," I replied, surprised by such a kind, warm invitation. He seemed like a genuinely nice person with no ulterior motive and I felt quite safe in his company.

"We're about to get a bite to eat now, at the grill stand over there. Their *Pinchos* are really special. Would you like to try some?" He was grinning like a boy about to open a big bar of chocolate. How could I resist?

"Sure, why not?" I accepted, smiling back. "Everyone here is so friendly and fun. I love the atmosphere".

"Yes, I know!" he agreed enthusiastically. I followed him to meet Ben, who seemed even more excited about the delicious food on offer.

The two guys made friendly banter which I found thoroughly entertaining and enjoyed listening to their delightful accents. We sat down at one of the plastic picnic tables set out beside the big mobile restaurant stand and I gladly let them choose from the menu for me. It seemed they had been there before and knew exactly which tasty treats were best.

Pete and I sat across from each other, whilst Ben did most of the talking, and I couldn't help but notice my dancing partner's vivid blue eyes. They hid shyly behind his glasses but seemed to sparkle every time he spoke to me. I was beginning to like Mr Happy Face and his smiling, gentle and unassuming manner.

Afterwards, we all walked around the town together, visiting the other music spots, before returning to the square to meet with a few of their Spanish friends. And later, Pete and I both wore delighted grins as we danced to more booming Latin rhythms together. I enjoyed the group's company till, at last, we were all quite tired and it was time to leave the party. It had turned into a wonderful night of music, dancing for hours, meeting new people and having fun conversations.

Mr Happy Face said good night to his buddy and insisted on walking me to my hotel. We chatted amiably, like old friends, all the way back. Standing outside the door, we agreed to meet the next day to watch the big parade; a grand carnival finale through the streets of the town.

"I guess you'll need my phone number? Then, we can find each other," I offered. As yet, he had made no attempt to ask for it. Normally, as a rule, I would never give out my number to a man unless I felt very sure that he was trustworthy.

"No, you take mine," he replied. "It's better that way."

This was something I was not used to. Most men would grab the opportunity. "But why not? Let me give you mine," I said, feeling a little confused.

"Well…er… it's because… then you can call me… if you really want to," he said awkwardly.

"Sure, I want to. But if you have my number, you can call me, too. Didn't we just agree to go to tomorrow's parade together?" I said, still not understanding his reasoning. So, I got out my phone, took his number as he suggested, and gave him a missed call.

"There, that was easy," I said smiling. "Now we both have each other's number." I thanked him for walking me back and bid him goodnight.

He gave me a little peck on the cheek, smiled and turned away, saying, "Hasta luego," over his shoulder as he disappeared up the hill. Well, I thought, he was certainly not the kind of man I was used to.

It was wonderful to just be herself, thought the princess. At last, she could proudly stand in all her glorious frogginess without putting on any airs. She knew that she didn't need a prince to complete her and could equally have had fun on her own. Although, her Prince Charming may have come along, he was not the reason for her radiance. Well, perhaps, his blue eyes *added to her sparkle but it was her own inner contentment that glowed brightly and held **him** captivated – no magic potions necessary.*

It wasn't until the next morning that I received the text message he'd sent only minutes after leaving me the night before. It was short and sweet, saying that he was very happy to have met me and was looking forward to tomorrow. Of course, I was thrilled but waited till I had finished my brunch before replying. I was sitting in a cafe across the street from the hotel as I re-worded the text several times so that I didn't sound too eager. I sent my first message to Pete but there was no immediate response. Perhaps he was still sleeping, I reassured myself. I had to be patient, as back then, standard text messages via international lines would often take much longer to get through to each other's mobile phones.

Later that afternoon, I followed the crowds through the town for the grand parade. I still had not received a reply from Mr Happy Face and was trying not to feel disheartened. In the distance, I could hear the drums of the carnival begin resonating as the party atmosphere returned to the streets. This time, there were much bigger crowds, around the little town, lining the parade route. I found myself standing on the steps of an entertainment arcade with gaming machines. It was a good spot as I could see over the heads of the people in front and watch the first fabulous floats begin to drift past.

"What if I misunderstood? He still hasn't answered my text message from this morning. Did he say we'd meet at the square or somewhere else? Perhaps he has changed his mind?" I thought, feeling anxious and checking my phone for messages again. It was now around three in the afternoon, the parade had begun but there was still no sign of the guys.

Inge, my dragon, had been plaguing me all day and had me thinking that Mr Happy Face was just another 'one-time wonder'. "You're probably not his type. He was just having fun last night and he was just feeling sorry for you because you're alone," it hissed. I tried not to think about Pete and ignored the dragon's wicked whispers. "I must go back to just enjoying my own company," I told myself but was failing miserably.

The music and noise were so loud that I could hardly hear my own thoughts. I needed a quiet place to talk to Fae, so I went inside to the arcade's toilets. I sat on the seat and closed my eyes, taking a few deep breaths and tried to relax. I didn't want my anxiety to spoil my peaceful, happy holiday. "Should I just forget it and give up the idea of seeing him again? Or should I text him again? I really don't want to send lots of texts and make him think I'm pushy. Fae, tell me please, what I should do?" I pleaded.

She answered immediately. "Stop worrying. If that is what you want, do it. Just text him."
But that would be totally against my dating rules, I thought. "Oh, I just don't know. What if... what if he isn't that interested in me? If I start chasing him, he might think I'm easy and lose interest."
"You're not chasing or being pushy. Stop dithering! If you want to talk to him, just do it. You've nothing to lose." Fae was making herself very clear.
"Okay, okay... I'll do it," I agreed and wrote a short, 'non-pushy' message to Pete. After re-reading it a couple of times, I pressed send thinking nothing would come of it, and went back outside again.

He replied instantly, saying they, too, were at the carnival and asking where I was. I was surprised and overjoyed, perhaps a little more than I should have been. I looked up and down the street, trying to figure out how to describe my location. Moments later, the phone rang as I was writing my next reply. It seemed he couldn't wait for my text to arrive and decided to call instead. We tried to talk but I could hardly hear anything above the music and noise. It was so loud that I was having trouble hearing him even after going back inside the toilets.

"Okay. I will find you. No problem," he shouted after I'd tried to describe my location.
"But why don't I come to you? We can meet in the same place as last night, in the square," I shouted back.
"No, that's okay. Don't go anywhere. I will find you. I'll be five minutes," he insisted.
I decided not to argue.
"Just let *him* find you," whispered Fae.
After the call, I sent another message to confirm that my location was in front of the Maritime Hotel, on the steps of the Casino Club.
"Very unusual for someone who is supposedly not interested in me," I thought, banishing Inge back to the dungeons. It certainly wasn't cheap to call mobile to mobile when abroad. Once more, I was pleasantly surprised by Mr Happy Face. "I guess he must have been busy earlier," I decided, wondering why I had got myself so worked up and anxious. "Thanks again, Fae."

The parade wound its way along the esplanade, then around several streets going through the town and eventually, down to the central square. Five minutes turned into ten, then thirty and then an hour had passed by, throughout which Pete and I continued to exchange messages and telephone calls, trying to communicate my location. Meanwhile, a very patient Ben was being dragged around by his rather determined friend, who continued searching up and down the streets and through the hoards of people, looking for 'some girl'. It certainly wasn't easy to get through those jostling masses but Pete wasn't going to give up.

I remained firmly in my spot, watching the floats and dancing processions go by whilst keeping a close eye on passers-by in case the two guys missed me. At that time, we didn't have the Internet, maps or satellite navigation on our phones, so I placed my trust in Fae's advice.

Finally, as the last few jangling music troupes marched past and the crowds began to dissipate, I saw two familiar figures in the distance walking towards me. We greeted each other warmly like old friends and laughed about the whole comical situation. Apparently, there was another Maritime Hotel at the other end of town, along with another casino venue nearby.

"Come on – let's get a coffee," invited Pete, with that irresistible happy face again.
"Oh, yes! You must try this very special coffee they have here. We can go to our favourite cafe," added Ben, who continued to entertain us with his love of food and off-beat humour for the rest of the afternoon. Sitting inside the chic little cafe across from the two men, I felt Pete's twinkling, blue- eyed gaze upon me again. He seemed to speak much less than Ben but was clearly the leader of the two. What he lacked in wit and humour, he more than made up for in warmth, quiet confidence and interestingly, great persistence.

Later, the princess and her new found friends all met again at the main square for more fun, laughter, music and dancing. The smiling prince was quietly winning her affections and had generously invited her to join them for the rest of the holiday. The two gentlemen were planning to take trips up to the mountains and see many other sites, and they warmly invited her. And so, the princess happily accepted, knowing she was in safe hands.

On the second night of the ball, the two danced again, delighting in the synchronicity of their movements, both exhilarated by the Latin rhythms. They danced is if they had danced together for years and did not stop till almost dawn.

When at last, the others had all gone and they were weary, the two took a gentle stroll to enjoy the refreshing rush of sea air. They walked, talked and watched the waves crash onto the rocks. It was, indeed, a night of enchantment.

An Extraordinary Prediction

Having only had a couple of hours sleep, my over-excited brain thought it would be a good idea to wake up ridiculously early and replay all the events of the last few days. It was now the fourth day of my holiday which was turning out to be much more fun than I'd ever expected. Despite being exhausted, I couldn't go back to sleep and I was still trying to process all that had happened, so I decided to go down for breakfast. "Perhaps if I eat something, it'll help me sleep again. Especially, if I'm going to see Mr Happy Face and have another fun-packed day today, I need to recharge". Whilst getting dressed and ready, I looked in the mirror and found myself grinning incessantly. Obviously, my efforts at trying to push aside thoughts about Pete were failing.

Half an hour later, back in my hotel room, I sat on the windowsill, looking out into the dreary little courtyard. I had sneaked out a cup of tea from the dining room and was enjoying one cigarette before going back to bed. "Budget hotels don't afford much of a view," I thought, "but it doesn't matter. I am having an absolutely amazing time!"

My heart was feeling full and happy again, knowing I was doing exactly what I wanted at this moment in my life. Although I had planned on having a holiday of solitude, both Pete and Ben were great company and we all seemed to be getting along great together. "Thank you for this place, this little hotel and keeping me safe. And thank you for the music, dancing, fun and laughter," I said looking up towards the small patch of blue sky above. "And of course, thank you for this wonderful encounter and letting me meet the lovely Mr Happy Face."

After a while, feeling very tired, I got into bed and was ready to drift off. As I took a few deep breaths and became deeply relaxed, I and continued my thoughts of heartfelt gratitude. Upon arriving at my peaceful place, Fae showed up as usual but it seemed she was anxious to tell me something.

"So, you think you had nothing to do with making this happen?" she smiled, referring to my meeting Pete.
"Of course, I did not!" I answered defensively.
"But it is exactly that, which you wished for. Remember the perfect man story you wrote?" said Fae calmly.
"No, no, it can't be. That thing didn't work. As I told you before the holiday, I absolutely do not want another holiday romance. All I wanted was a nice, uneventful little holiday, just to regenerate my energy," I argued. "Anyway, nothing significant has really happened between us."
"Yes, but don't you remember? I told you there would be big changes," Fae said. She could be very insistent at times. "I did try to tell you about him. Remember, that vision... with the stranger?"

Suddenly, as if an electric shock had gone through me, I sat bolt upright in bed, eyes wide open. "What?! NO WAY!" I exclaimed aloud as my memory clicked into place. "OH, MY GOD! You've got to be kidding!" The whole scene came rushing back to me and sent my mind racing. Until that moment, I had completely forgotten the vision. "How can that be?" I gasped, astounded at my realisation. "That distant stranger I met in my meditations? No, no, it can't be him – can it? Is it really him?" I was utterly flabbergasted.

As you know, just a few months before, Fae had tried to introduce me to a man during my meditation and I had refused. A few weeks later, he had appeared again, still as a dark shadowy figure standing in the distance. Although I had sensed he was friendly, I dismissed him once more, telling Fae very firmly that I simply was not ready or interested.

Yet again, another two weeks later, he appeared for the third time in my meditation, waiting patiently in the distance. "Just go and say hello. That's all I'm asking," urged Fae.
"Really, must I? But it's not what I need right now. Can't we just focus on my career and manifesting a new job?" After I had been made redundant, the last thing I wanted or needed was to think about getting into a relationship.
"It won't hurt to say hello," she persisted.
"Okay, okay, I'm going," I said grudgingly and moved closer to the figure. Although, I couldn't see him clearly, I sensed a warm, loving presence. His face was not clear but all I perceived were those bright blue eyes and a broad smile. He held out his hands in a warm welcome and as I took them, he said, "I am coming to see you soon. Wait for me."

My mind was racing, I wanted to ask so many questions such as 'Who are you? What is your name? How will I know you?' but I couldn't formulate the words. Instead, I simply asked, "Where are you from?"
"Germany," he answered and turned to leave, saying, "I must fly." Again, he beamed that warm, loving, smile upon me and disappeared through a door.
When I turned back to Fae, she seemed very pleased and said excitedly, "He's the one! You're going to meet him soon." I was not at all keen on the idea but thanked her anyway.

"Yeah, great. How ridiculous," I thought, after coming out of the meditation. "Obviously, my imagination was going into overdrive again.

And where, exactly, am I going to meet a *German* guy? At the salsa club? At the supermarket or perhaps, the post office? Highly unlikely." Soon afterwards, I wasted little time thinking about the vision and dismissed it, deciding it was probably just an old default programme that I still needed to work on. Anyway, I had far more important things to worry about.

Now, just a few weeks later, here I am in my hotel room, on this island, at carnival time, having met the man I had seen in my vision – unbelievable! As the puzzle pieces fell into place, the reality of what was happening began to dawn on me. I remembered everything Fae had said and my impressions about that person; his warm, bright smile and those unmistakeable blue eyes. Pete was, indeed, German. When he had said, "I must fly," he did not mean, "I must go" but he was alluding to his profession. He had been in the Air Force for many years and his current business revolved around his passion for aviation. It was all making sense. That stranger in my meditations was not just a whim of my creative brain but a genuine precognitive vision, a forecast about my future.

As comprehension swept over me, I was overwhelmed and tears started rolling down my face. "You said… I'm sure you told me… that, that he would be the *one*! Is Pete the one? Now? Here? Finally?" I tried to talk with Fae but my heart was racing and I couldn't connect or relax enough to hear her voice because of the commotion inside my head.

In the past, my tears had always expressed anguish, sadness and frustration. But now I was overcome with so many emotions; utter joy, disbelief, surprise and in absolute awe of how I had tapped into this magic. These tears were coming from a huge sense of gratitude and gladness for having at last, arrived. I wanted to sing and jump for joy! Divine intervention had, indeed, stepped in to ensure that I would be here at this particular moment in time and made our paths cross.

Last night, when the carnival party was over and the crowds had gone, Pete and I had walked around town and sat, talking until the early hours. It was wonderful and amazing getting to know each other. I found it simply astounding how his values, beliefs and ways of thinking uncannily matched mine. It was not only the love of Latin culture, music and dancing that we had in common but also our life expectations and dreams were almost identical. Over the days together, I would discover more and more similarities such as our understanding of religion, spirituality, worldviews, attitudes towards family, work ethics and so on. It was as though we had been made in the same kitchen from the same ingredients and came out of the same mould.

Being with Pete was nothing like being with anyone else I had ever known. Although we could talk for hours, no words were actually necessary to feel the connection; it was effortless and one of total trust and perfect ease. Some years after leaving the ships, my good friend Cherie had met her soon-to-be-husband and we were discussing how she knew he was the 'one'. "Being with the right person should be as easy as breathing," she had described and of course, she was right. The fake princess was long gone and no feminine wiles, charms or card playing were necessary. The shoe fitted perfectly, simply by being me and my authentic self.

I remembered all that I had written about in my perfect relationship story just a year and half ago. "That's impossible!" I thought. "How on Earth can *this* happen!" The more I discovered about Pete, the more he seemed to fit *exactly* as I had described. I was utterly awestruck by how powerful my magical mind tools had worked.

I felt incredulous, excited and hopeful that, at last, I had found the *one*. But I also felt soothed with a sense of peace and contentment, knowing that the space in my heart would no longer be empty. It was now clear that what I had always suspected and believed deep down, despite all that I had been through, was indeed, true; that if I existed on this planet, somewhere out there, so did he, my soul partner.

At the same time, I was overwhelmed as I realised that all through my journey I had been taken care of, that there was a reason for everything I'd experienced. My heart and mind had connected with the forces of nature and the search was at long last, over.

However, along with this awareness, there came the next hurdle. "Oh, no, no, no!" I wrestled with my emotions as I realised that we would be going home in just a few days and I might never see him again! Inge reappeared and seized the chance, reminding me of other failed holiday romances. Although I had healed my broken heart and conquered many of my fears, I had not yet mastered how to befriend my dragon. Anxiety and worry started to creep into my joy-filled revelations. "What should I do?"
Fae's response was instantaneous: "Just trust," she said.

Eventually, the tiredness took over and I fell into a restless slumber. When I awoke, it was early afternoon but the worries continued. Keeping my eyes closed, I tried to calm my scattered mind using positive affirmations. Again, Fae was there to help and whispered soothingly, "Don't think about the past, my dear. This time it's very different. No need to be anxious. You don't have to *do* anything. He loves you."

"Really? How can I know that?" I asked, finding it hard to believe that he might *love* me already. "He hasn't done anything to show it. He doesn't behave like most men. I don't know if he is actually interested in me or just being friendly."
"Oh, hasn't he?" Fae continued soothingly. "Then, who searched for hours through the crowds at the parade and didn't give up till he found you? And who wanted to be with you and didn't want you to feel alone?

Why should he want to share with *you* all that he knows and loves about this island?" She was right of course, as always.

"Yes, I suppose so," I conceded. "It's true, despite his shyness, Pete did ask me to join him and his friends." It reminded me of the old saying that 'actions speak louder than words' and, in his case, it meant doing things together.

If Mr Happy Face was indeed, her prince, she must be the luckiest lady in the land, thought the princess. Her fairy godmother had done all she could to ensure that she would go to the ball and dance till dawn. Well, it was certainly the most romantic event ever a girl could imagine! The princess was very grateful, of course. Now, it was up to her to make her dream come true.

But she was also, afraid that it might only be a dream, for the prince was more than she had ever hoped for. As yet, she had only encountered the very surface of her prince's onion and was worried that he too might turn out to be a toad. Alas, she knew that she was running out of time on this enchanted island. Perhaps, this is all she would have and must treasure these precious moments forever.

The rest of our holiday was spent travelling around, meeting more of his friends, soaking up the culture and seeing some fascinating sites together. Although it was Pete's first time at the carnival, he had been to the island many times before and seemed to know it well. My original plans for journaling, sketching and sitting on a rock were all completely cast aside. Spending time with the two guys was simply, more fun. It somehow felt as though we had always been good friends when the three of us were together. And at the end of each night, Pete would be the perfect gentleman and walk me back to my hotel.

As the days wore on, I was still worried about my revelation and dearly wanted to talk openly with Pete about it. Of course, he had no notion of Fae's guidance and my intuitive or manifesting abilities. However, I knew that if I were to disclose any of those thoughts too soon, he might think I was completely mad and it could scare him away forever. The secret behind our magical encounter would have to be kept quiet for now. I needed to gain his trust first. Meanwhile, Pete was blissfully unaware of the tumult going inside me... or that I had fallen head over heels in love with him.

I decided it was best to trust in the process as Fae had advised, and be content to just bask in the gentle warmth and friendly companionship of just being with him. Every moment together became precious as I had no idea what might happen once we would return to our respective countries. I decided to simply be grateful for the time together with the occasional hug or surreptitious handholding which, according to Fae, meant much more than I had realised.

Spending time with Pete was so very different from any relationship I had previously experienced. It is difficult to put into words just how easy and comfortable it was being in each other's company. It was perhaps akin to the feeling of being with a friend you've known forever. I could be myself completely without any façade, guardedness or formality. When we were together, I could simply *be*, in a way I had never been with anyone else before.

The seven days flew past far too quickly and yet, I felt as though I had been there for a month. Coincidently, as if the gods were taunting me, the two guys were due to fly home on the very same day as me and our flights were within half an hour of each other. Pete kindly offered that I join them for the drive to the airport and picked me up from my hotel.

Alas, Inge was revelling in churning up my emotions and filling my stomach with anxiety again. As yet, Pete had not mentioned a word about keeping in touch or wanting to see me again. This could be the very last time I would see this wonderful man! The man who might well be my destiny, my true life partner, the one I'd been searching for forever.

Whilst we were waiting in the airport lounge, I broke another one of my dating rules and wrote down all my phone numbers and contact details on a postcard and handed it to him. "This is for you. In case you want to contact me," I said, trying to be casual.
"Thank you. Yes, sure, I will." he said simply, with a bright smile and a warm hug. Then, continued talking about the planes we were watching outside.

The gods were definitely having fun because even our boarding gates were right beside each other. The two guys stood in their queue as I shuffled along in mine. As we waved goodbye, I continued to wear a jovial smile whilst hiding the anxiety and sadness. I was missing him already. On the plane, I settled down into my seat and breathed deeply, trying hard to calm my fretful heart. I sent him one last text message but didn't receive any reply. It was time to switch off my phone and go back to reality. Reaching for my tissues, I stared out of the window and allowed myself to release the emotions that I had been holding back.

As the plane reached altitude and the islands disappeared below, I closed my eyes and tried to hear Fae. I needed her reassurance and comforting words but a crowded plane, restless mind and miserable heart are not conducive to making intuitive connections. It was not until many hours later, when I was safely back home, tucked up in my own bed and just about to fall asleep, when she returned, whispering, "Don't stress, my dear. Let go of your worries. Just *trust* and believe. All will be well."

How Manifestation Works

My final lesson for you is about understanding the principles of manifestation and how to make it work for you. You might have heard the quote by Wayne Dyer, "You create your thoughts, your thoughts create your intentions and your intentions create your reality".[20] This is of course, true but the real secret lies in knowing *how* to create the *right* thoughts.

Changing your thoughts is only the beginning because manifesting your wishes encompasses much more than just positive thinking. Therefore, it is important to understand the stages and main factors required to make the manifestation process work well.

Once you are fully ready to manifest your true life partner, the one who matches you perfectly, you should learn the fundamental principles of this ancient, powerful art. It is essential to understand and integrate this knowledge, which can not only change your life, but also influence and benefit family, friends and others people in your circle.

Manifestation has always been present and working in your life but probably, you were not aware of it. Have you ever noticed that when someone is feeling good about something, he/she tends to attract more good things? For example, you might have experienced any of the following coincidental situations:

- You find a lucky penny, a four-leafed clover or perhaps you see a rainbow. You might believe good things come in threes or notice something else which you believe to be lucky. Then, more lucky things come into your reality, confirming your belief.

- You start dating someone new and feel incredibly happy. Then somehow, you seem to attract more hopeful candidates that take an interest in you, despite your being unavailable.
- You get a good score in a test, win at the lottery or in a competition, and your positivity and confidence spill over into other areas of your life, bringing more wins and success.
- You generously give some heartfelt attention to a friend, loved one or pet with no expectation of gaining anything in return. Later, you receive a favour or kindness from another unexpected source.

No doubt, you've experienced those days when things just feel good and everything seems to fall into place easily. Equally, there are those horrid days when the opposite seems to happen. Have you ever wondered why? Is it possible to create more of the good days? The answer is really quite simple – we create more of what we are *feeling most* of the time, not just how we *think*. This means, if you often feel good, you attract more things that make you feel good. And equally, if you regularly feel bad, you attract more bad things.

According to Abraham (Ester Hicks), you should, "Seek your vibrational alignment first, and then follow through with inspired action."[21] In other words, when we are in a state of happiness, contentment or appreciation, we can attract more of the same. First, we need to create these positive feelings and then take action based on positive, intuitive or inspired direction.

Just as a mobile phone or radio creates frequencies or waves of energy which we cannot see, our emotions generate measurable electromagnetic waves that fluctuate depending on our thoughts and feelings.[22] If we feel frustrated, angry, sad, fearful or any other negative emotion, we create slower and rather erratic frequencies. Positive feelings, however, such as being loving, joyful, grateful or compassionate produce faster, steadier, more coherent frequencies.[23]

Recent scientific 'heart-brain coherence' studies have shown that when the thoughts in our brains are congruent with the emotions in our hearts, we can actually create a powerful positive effect on what is happening inside ourselves, as well as the world around us.[24] This means, when our minds and our hearts are aligned, and we are *thinking* and *feeling* positive in the same way about something, we find that somehow, we attract luck and good things. Often, everything just tends to fall into place and the work, project, journey or whatever we might be working on, becomes much easier.

For instance, since healing and releasing all of my past relationship baggage, I was mostly in a state of contentment and satisfaction with my life, myself and everything that was happening. For several months before the holiday, I remember feeling glad and grateful for all that I had been through. By the time I got on the plane, I was very much at peace and centred within myself already. Hence, at that moment when I met Pete, my heart and mind were generating a healthy, positive frequency, which naturally attracted more of the same kind of healthy, balanced and good energy into my life.

If, on the other hand, I had gone on my holiday believing I was down on my luck, having lost my job and feeling sad, stressed or worried, I would have only attracted more of that same negative energy. If I had focused on having to be alone on that holiday and lacking a friend or partner to be with, as I might have felt in the past, I would have attracted more lack and loneliness. Therefore, if we can change our inner selves, our mood and mind, to be in a more positive state simultaneously, we will automatically attract more positive, healthy situations.

The first step in learning how to manifest anything, whether it is a new relationship, job, home or an opportunity, is to understand that you must change that on which your *thoughts* and *feelings* dwell on *most* of the time. If you find yourself stuck in a really negative mood, you can break out of it by doing something that makes you laugh. Simply watching a funny film or listening to a joke which makes you laugh out loud, can break the cycle and relieve your body and brain from the spiral of negative emotion for an instant. Then, you can do something to keep the raised frequency flowing by taking actions that create more ongoing, positive energy.

LESSON 9: Manifesting Principles

In the previous chapters, you learned how to change your thinking and beliefs. The following exercise will help you change your emotional state and become align these feelings with your positive thoughts.

A. Change Your Vibe Exercise

This is a short meditation exercise that you need to do thoroughly and only once.

1. As you did before, take the steps to relax, slow down and breathe deeply. Take your time to be calm and relax your whole mind and body.
2. In your mind, go to your peaceful place and then, into your special room.
3. On your screen, imagine seeing a special pet or someone you love deeply. Allow yourself to dwell on the positive emotions you feel for them. Take your time to feel love, kindness, appreciation and gratitude.
4. Imagine these emotions like a beautiful, warm glow inside your heart. See and feel this light as it glows brighter around your heart space. See it growing, increasing and expanding all around you. You can give it a colour.
5. Now, imagine taking this brilliant energy and pouring it into a big jar or bottle. Close the lid. You can imagine it is a gas or liquid inside the bottle. Know that it is full of healthy, positive, love-filled energy which never runs out. You might want to label your bottle with a name, like 'Elixir of Happiness' or 'Unconditional Love'.

6. Shrink the bottle and put it in your pocket. You can now carry it with you everywhere.
7. Come out from your meditation slowly in the usual way.

You can also refill your bottle with more positive emotions whenever you feel really good and have a positive, happy experience. Simply imagine topping up your bottle with the good emotions.

Next, whenever you feel low, worried or upset, you can now change your state easily by doing the following:

8. Acknowledge to yourself, the negative thoughts or feelings you are currently having. Admit these emotions aloud by saying a statement such as, "I am really annoyed about..." or "I feel stressed because of..."
9. Close your eyes and create an intention to change your state. Say words to yourself such as, "I now put these feelings and thoughts aside for a while. Instead, I choose to focus on more positive, productive and healthier feelings and thoughts." You might like to imagine putting the negative feelings and thoughts into a box, making it smaller and pushing it aside.
10. Now, imagine taking a drink from your Happiness Elixir bottle or pouring it over your head and being wrapped in its energy. As you do this, feel your heart filling up with those loving, compassionate, appreciative emotions. Imagine the positive emotions wash through you and replace any negative feelings. You can also focus on the person, pet or thing that makes you feel good.
11. Say this affirmation: "I completely trust and allow all good things to come into my life."

Please note: this method is not about diminishing the importance of your worries or forgetting your problems. On the contrary, by changing your emotional state, you change your vibrations, which will then give you a window of calm so that you can become centred. When you are not as overwhelmed with worry, stress or anxiety, you will be able to think clearly, be more creative, find solutions and take positive action with the issue at hand.

B. The Manifestation Process

In the previous chapters, I described some magical methods of manifestation such as the meditations and writing down the story of your perfect relationship. These methods are powerful because they employ particular principles that are imperative to the process and which I explain here in a little more detail. When these principles are combined and applied appropriately, they can multiply the efficacy of your manifestation.

One of the key factors in the manifestation process is to understand that 'like attracts like'. Contrary to the law of physics, such as magnetism where opposite poles attract, the reverse is true for the 'Law of Attraction'. With human interactions and relationships, we usually attract the same *energy* we emit. In other words, we must try to generate the kind of energy we want to attract from our potential partners, in ourselves first. We subliminally attract those people into our lives that are on similar *wavelengths* or energy frequencies as ourselves. This manifestation process will show you how to change your energy frequency so that you can attract the right person for you.

Whether it is a new relationship, moving house, attracting more customers or improving your wellbeing, you can apply this process to whatever you wish to manifest. The diagram in Figure 4 illustrates the four main principles and their elements.

Figure 4: The Manifestation Process

1. VISION

At the outset of any endeavour, it is crucial that you identify and clarify in your mind, exactly what you wish to manifest. The more precise you can be, the more likely you will recognise and receive it. If I had not written down my 'Perfect Partner' story in detail, I would not have paid much attention to Pete when he came along. Had I met him some years beforehand, I would most likely have dismissed the encounter as, on the surface, he seemed very different to the kind of man I would usually be attracted to. Creating an honest and genuine vision or goal for your desired perfect partner is the first essential step.

Your vision should include these elements:

- SPECIFIC: Create a clear and specific vision of your desires. You can do this in many ways such as meditation, mental visualisation, creating a vision board or writing it down. Whichever way you choose, it is essential that your vision has explicit, unambiguous details. Also, do not include what you do *not* want. Many people describe their wishes in the negative (e.g., "I don't want to live alone anymore," instead of saying, "I want to live with my life partner"). The subconscious focuses on whatever you give it, and if you think about your desire in negative terms, you will manifest more of the negative.

- DESIRE+EMOTION: Ensure you really *feel* the emotion of your true desire as you visualise. This does not mean you should feel a desperate hunger and longing for your future partner. Also, it does not mean that you should get down on your knees and beg God with tears in your eyes. That kind of emotion only creates more of the feeling of lacking a partner in your life. The secret is in imagining that this beautiful relationship *is already yours* and creating the feeling of it being in existence now with genuine, heartfelt emotion and *gratitude*. Visualise this feeling of absolute happiness and fill your heart with gladness for all that you already have.

- AFFIRMATION: Reaffirm your desired vision regularly in your mind whenever you are calm and relaxed. An easy way to do this is by writing down a positive affirmation such as, "I am extremely glad and grateful to be in a perfect relationship with my Mr/Ms Right." Write this on a sticky note and place it where you will see it often.

Now, combine these three elements whenever you read your affirmation by allowing yourself to feel the feelings deeply and at the same time, visualise the happy-ever-after image in your mind. The best time to do this is every morning upon waking and at night before sleeping. Doing this whilst you are relaxed will embed these thoughts into your subconscious mind. Practise this simple mental affirmation of your dream, vision or goal for at least a month.

2. ACTION

Plan a course of action to create more inner happiness which will attract to you all that is good and all that you deserve in life. I am sure you are familiar with writing lists of to-dos and creating action plans for home or work projects. However, it is not often we do this for our own personal development.

Please understand that by taking action, I do not mean you should set out on a partner-hunting mission and join lots of dating sites or attend every social event in full pursuit, with all guns blazing, trying to find the elusive Mr/Ms Right. This is not necessary. Once you have done the Making Magic exercises as described in Chapter 9, let it go and simply focus on your own happiness and health. Creating more happiness and freedom in your heart, body and mind is the key to attracting the love you seek.

- PLAN: Create a self-care plan that will turn you into a 'magnet' that generates the kind of energy you wish to attract. In other words, do the things that make you feel happy, centred and complete. It does not matter whether the activities are at work or in your own time as long as they nurture your mind, body and spirit, and therefore, raise your positive frequency. You can do this by listening to your inner voice/IGS and writing down a list of all the possible things that lifts your spirit and makes you smile or feel alive. Note down some simple, tangible steps of what, where and when you might want to do these activities.

- POSITIVE ACTION: Make time to do these activities regularly, at least once or twice a week. When you do the things you love often, it is the best way to regenerate your batteries and nurture every level of your being. Anything that increases your inner happiness – such as taking a walk, enjoying nature, being creative, doing a hobby, sport/exercise or joining a club or society that makes you feel invigorated – is a perfect way to raise your happiness level.

- SELF NURTURE: Whether you are in a relationship or not, making positive choices that raise your sense of fulfilment and self-worth are essential. Make a habit of taking regular actions that increase your inner confidence and self-esteem. This will keep you from hankering for happiness from outside of yourself. Other people cannot make you happy; it is only when your cup is full and overflowing that it will spill into the cups of those who are dear to you. You can also do this by using the affirmations listed in the next exercise to create a mindset that accepts, cares for and celebrates all that is you.

As you do things to nurture yourself and become more self-aware and self-loving, you will feel more contented inside, and therefore, raise your frequency to attract your soul partner and align with her/him on a deeper, subconscious level. When you are happy on the inside, life brings you more things to be happy about from the outside.

However, self-love does not mean becoming too self-sufficient or totally independent which will only send out the signal that your heart is closed and there is no room for another person. If you often think and say words such as, "I can manage fine on my own" and "I don't need/want a man/woman for anything", then reconsider the intention behind those words and whether you are actually saying what you *truly* feel. Is your heart and mind being coherent? Self-love means having enough love, acceptance and compassion towards yourself, so that you have a deep sense of completeness, in not just being *who* you are, but also being open to letting others into your heart.

3. RELEASE

It is now time to let go and trust in the process. Firstly, if you haven't done so already, begin by releasing, grieving and forgiving all the residual pain and attachments from your past as suggested in Chapters 3, 7 and 8. It was only after I had finally healed the wounds and forgiven my past that my heart became open to attracting a new, much healthier and happier relationship.

- RELEASE DESIRE: You have now healed the past and let go of all the unnecessary programmes and patterns from previous relationships. You have also done the visualisation and manifestation exercises, as explained in Chapter 9, and affirmed your desire for at least a month. Having done all the hard work and developed the habit of taking action to nurture your spirit, it is now time to let go and release this wanting or desire from your *conscious* mind.

This is a necessary step in the art of manifestation as it gives your subconscious mind the chance to do its job.

Releasing desire does not mean that you no longer want to find Ms/Mr Right but simply that you let go of the 'hunger' or 'longing' you used to feel. You might think this sounds contrary and you should actively chase your dream. However, you must now accept that you are at the point of having done all that is necessary and you can let go of the *doing*. In other words, stop dwelling on *wanting* that relationship all the time and just *be*. The door is not closed but remains open, only you are not running outside the door and grabbing every stranger that walks by.

The principle of releasing desire is akin to placing your order at a restaurant. We can usually imagine how a dish will look and taste whilst we are selecting our meal from the menu. Once we have decided and can be very specific about our choice, knowing exactly how we want our meal to be, we place our order. Then, we sit back and wait patiently, trusting the kitchen to create our order to the best of their ability. We know that it will be delivered *when* it is ready. As in any good restaurant, it is essential to trust the chef and be patient, knowing that your order will be properly prepared and arrive in good time. But if you are impatient and keep checking on the kitchen, not only will you distrust the chef, you will also disturb the cooking process.

If it helps, you can imagine this step as releasing your wishes to the forces of nature by mentally putting all of those thoughts, desires and feelings in a box and placing it on a shelf in your mind. Or, if you are spiritual or religious, you may want to place it in the hands of a higher power and trust that your request is being taken care of.

- RELEASE EXPECTATION: We often get locked into our expectations of how the thing or person we really want should be. As you have already affirmed that you will only attract the right partner, now you must let go of how, when and where this will happen. Allow yourself to surrender the need to control any superfluous expectations and simply believe and trust in the process, knowing that whatever comes will be what is best for you.

I know I said that you must be detailed and precise in your vision at the outset but there is one caveat to this plan: when your wish is eventually granted, it could arrive in a different package than you might have expected. This is not to say you must accept any and all candidates that show up and of course, you can be as discerning as you wish to be in your choices. For instance, your perfect partner may show up in the most unlikely place, under a different guise or title and at a time you least expect. The secret is that he/she may not look or seem anything like the person you expected but the way they make you *feel* will be just as you envisioned.

I had to learn to throw out my 'rule book' which meant to stop expecting a man to look or act in a particular way. Initially, Pete was not as forward in making his feelings known to me, and in the past, I would have interpreted that as a lack of interest. He had also been in the Air Force, which I was vehemently against, and I would never have dated a 'military type'. But of course, Fae knew better, as Pete turned out to be nothing like the stereotypes I had imagined. So, I learned to keep an open mind and let go of unnecessary expectations.

- TRUST AND PATIENCE: When you release your desire and those unimportant expectations, you naturally begin to practice greater *patience* and *trust*. When you surrender and step back from consciously dwelling on your perfect partner, you must trust that your wishes have been registered and your unconscious mind is working on it. Now, you can relax, let go and simply enjoy being you. It is better to focus on your own happiness, do what you love and celebrate your life as it is, whilst remaining open in your heart. You can do this with the self-care activities mentioned before.

Stay centred and be patient with yourself, knowing that all will come to you in good time and in perfect synchronicity. If you truly *believe* there really exists a Mr/Ms Right who is perfect and also, looking for you, somewhere out there amongst the billions of people on this planet, then your thoughts will create that reality.

Now, if you feel that you have done all that you can but the manifestation process is taking much too long, perhaps it is worth considering that your perfect partner is not quite ready yet and still doing some work on healing herself/himself. Trust that the wheels are in motion and your magnetic, heartfelt energy is doing all that is necessary in order to align you with your perfect partner.

My clients have sometimes reported that their wishes came true almost immediately after shifting their thinking and letting go of old expectations or just by stopping negative self-talk. Others have said the perfect person arrived months later, once they had done the deeper self-work and released their old baggage. But in every case, the client was overwhelmed by how amazingly good the connection was and relationship has been since.

4. GRATITUDE

Probably, the most important principle in the art of manifesting is to maintain a deep sense of gratitude. In simple terms, this means being thankful every day for everything in your life. This is because the feeling of gratitude raises your frequency to the level that attracts love, abundance, happiness and more of the things that you can be grateful for.

Now, you may say, "But I am thankful already," which no doubt, you are. However, this principle is about living in a 'state' of thankfulness on a different level. Of course, I don't mean that you should go around saying thank you all day to every living and non-living thing that you come across. It is not necessary for you to say it out loud all the time.

Therefore, it is perhaps, helpful to first clarify what exactly I mean by gratitude. The English language includes the word 'you' along with 'thanks', which assumes that you must thank someone else instead of simply being thankful. Therefore, the act of *being thankful* does not require you to say anything to anyone but to simply *feel* a sense of appreciation and gladness in your heart.

- APPRECIATION: It is easy to be grateful for the good things that come our way such as receiving a gift or favour from someone or enjoying a happy event. However, we rarely feel thankful for things going wrong, the stressful situations or annoying people that we have to contend with. On the contrary, we feel upset or resentful for these difficulties. Yet, these are our greatest gifts as they bring about necessary change and learning.

    Now, you might think that if you are grateful for such awful things, it will invite more of them into your life but actually, the opposite is true. If you can change your negative thoughts to appreciative ones, especially during those difficult experiences, you will change the energy they have upon you and hence, diffuse the situation. As you become more accepting, you will have the chance to stop their nasty affects and be less stressed which will allow you to create a more positive outcome. By practising the feeling of gratitude for all that happens in your life, especially the difficult situations, you release their hold on you emotionally.

    A great way to practise gratitude is by keeping a 'gratitude journal', in which you write about things you are grateful for every day. If you find this difficult, try remembering things that happened in the past, good and bad, from which you have learned something and simply be glad for them.

- RECEIVE: Another often overlooked element in the principles of manifestation is that of 'receiving'. We often forget – or perhaps, never learned – *how* to receive what we rightly deserve, especially those of us whose default programme is to always give, support and take care of others. Please understand that receiving does not mean 'being entitled' or taking things for granted. It is quite the contrary and more about being whole-heartedly grateful and *open* to receive. I would never have been able to get those very precise precognitions if I hadn't been open and ready to receive them.

  For instance, how often has someone paid you a compliment to which you have reacted in a way that diminished your worth? Perhaps when someone gives you a gift, your immediate response is to think about what you should give back? It is almost as though we are embarrassed to receive and need to find reasons or excuses for it. Instead, just as a small child would, you could simply receive the compliment or gift with joy and gratitude. When you are open to receiving, you will begin the flow of energy to attract more good things into your life, just as generously as you are at giving of yourself.

  In order to manifest a relationship of giving and receiving love, we simply need to change our mindset. You can do this by cultivating an attitude of self-love which accepts that you *deserve* all that is good, equally, just as much as the next person. Simply close your eyes, place a hand on your heart and take a deep breath. Then, imagine there is a bright light glowing and growing inside your heart space. You might like to imagine a feeling of immense gratitude for any deeply loving relationship you already have or had in your life. Say to yourself, "My heart is now opening to receive more happiness and love". Let this feeling of gratitude and openness increase and dwell in it as long as you like.

- CELEBRATE: You have almost reached the end of this book, and I hope you are already reaping the benefits from the changes you have made. Now, after all the hard work you have done on healing your heart, you have earned some well-deserved 'fun time'. A good way to be in a state of gratitude and appreciation is to make time to celebrate all that it means to be you. For example, you can show yourself appreciation and gratitude by giving yourself a suitable 'reward' that makes you feel proud for all you have achieved so far, on this journey.
It is always beneficial to get into the habit of celebrating your small wins as it rewires your brain and emotions to feel that you are worthy, loved and appreciated. The rewards do not need to be big things and you do not need to spend any money. Simply taking a short walk in nature and appreciating the scenery is a wonderful way to refresh and thank yourself. I like to reward myself whenever I have accomplished particular tasks or overcome small hurdles by giving myself some well-deserved 'me time' and doing more of the things I love.

Being grateful can become a simple daily habit; for example, when you switch on the computer or use your mobile phone, feel thankful because you can use these amazing devices. As you read this book, you might feel glad that you have eyes to see it and have learned how to read. Or when you go about your day, be grateful for the food in your belly and clean water in the bathroom. When you simply take notice of the little things and feel gratitude, the bigger things will naturally come. The more glad and grateful we are, the more good things we will receive to be grateful for.

C. Regular Affirmations

A very simple and easy manifestation tool, which my clients and I regularly use, with amazing results, is the use of 'positive affirmations'. When you combine meditation and the manifestation process alongside the regular practice of affirmations, you will witness incredible changes, some of which are beyond explanation.

As I have mentioned previously, you should say your affirmations using the past or present tense. They must use positive words that state what you want, not what you don't want, and create the feeling of it having happened already.

Here are some more positive affirmations for you to select from. Simply write them by hand on a piece of paper or sticky note and place it beside your bed, in your wallet, next to your mirror or anywhere you will see it often. Read and say the words, aloud or to yourself, regularly:

- My heart has healed and is ready for profound happiness.
- I open my heart to receiving all that is good, healthy and happy.
- Thank you for all the past relationships; they have helped me learn and grow.
- I easily understand and follow the guidance that my IGS/soul/intuitive mind is giving me.
- I always make good decisions and take the right actions.
- I am utterly happy to have found and be with my wonderful Mr/Ms Right – thank you!
- I am my best, authentic self when I am with him/her.
- We match and understand each other perfectly.

- My life partner loves me just the way I am and I love her/him just the way he/she is.
- We have both found everything we ever wanted from a relationship with each other.
- I only attract that which is healthy/good/beneficial for myself and him/her.
- Our relationship is better than I ever imagined.
- My life is filled with love, happiness and abundance.

Also, don't forget to fill your affirmations and visualisations with good feelings and happy emotions. Always remember that when you say these words to yourself, be sure to feel gratitude and appreciation.

At the end of my story, what have we learned? Did I become fully healed from all the old wounds and hurt from my past? Was I able to eliminate all the negative default programmes? Had I wiped the slate clean and started with an untainted, new heart? Had my dragon completely disappeared and stopped sabotaging me? The answer to these questions, as I am sure you can guess, is no. My heart still has some scars and sometimes I have to poke Inge with the broom for not behaving. Those painful experiences will always remain in my memory archives but they no longer plague me. Some of the negative patterns occasionally show their cheeky faces but when they do, I am aware and can choose whether to humour them.

When it comes to love and relationships, we just need to remember that we are all constantly growing, changing and evolving. If we are open to loving and learning together, as we go along, we do not need to be perfect in order to have the perfect relationship.

My past history is part of who I am and I am glad and grateful for all that I have ever experienced. However, that history does not determine my present or future anymore. I have learned to love, accept and respect myself, just as I am, with my scars, warts and all. The greatest lesson for me was in learning my true worth, not just intellectually, but truly digesting, feeling and living by it. Once I changed my beliefs at the root level, only then could I attract the right kind of man. First, I had to allow my authentic self to shine in order to attract an equally authentic soul.

The nine lessons I have given you are, by no means comprehensive, but I sincerely hope that this guide will help you to heal deeply, live in your own wholeness and find that beautiful, fulfilling relationship you've always known was meant for you. Now, go – create your own fairy tale, make magic! And don't forget to write and tell me all about it.

Coming Home

Three days had passed since coming home from my extraordinary holiday. During the whole trip, I had not written a single word in my journal or done any sketching. "So much for rest, rumination and realignment," I thought as I sat up in bed at night, trying to meditate. My heart and mind were still whirling with all that had happened. "How could I have had such a fantastic connection, the most beautiful romantic experience with this a wonderful soul, and now be back here at home, sitting alone, as if nothing happened? After thirty-odd years of searching, I finally meet Mr Right – supposedly the one – only to find that he lives in another country and I'll probably never see him again," I thought, unhappily.

"He didn't ask to see me again when we said our goodbyes at the airport," I thought, still feeling confused. "How can I know if Pete was *actually* interested in me?"
"Just trust, my dear. I told you he is not like the others," said Fae.
"Well, he hasn't tried to get in touch at all – no calls, no texts, no emails." Having heard nothing, I was feeling quite disappointed and still missing him. I could not make sense of that vision, my premonition, and why it had all happened.
"Just have patience," said Fae. "Trust".
"Trust, trust! Yeah, that's what you always say," I said, exasperated. "Well, I *am* trusting and being patient. How long am I supposed to wait?"
"As long you want to wait. It's up to you," said Fae patiently.
"Oh, really? Up to me – what do you mean? Isn't the man supposed to do the chasing? I thought the rule was simple; if he doesn't show an obvious interest, then he's not interested."
"It's high time to throw out that rulebook and follow your gut instincts," said Fae firmly.

Indeed, the old patterns had grown threadbare but they still pulled hard at times. I could feel Inge waiting on the sidelines, still trying to provoke me into thinking the worst. Having had hardly any success in the past, it was easy to doubt my own intuition about men and relationships.

"The rulebook?" I knew what she meant but was reluctant to admit it. I had carefully cultivated these 'must dos and methods' of dating over the decades which usually worked. It was hard to just let them go.
"Forget the rules," repeated Fae. "Your typical dating rules are not relevant anymore. If you want to call him, call him. If you want to talk, just talk. It's simple; communicate." As a coach, I knew that the best way to solve any confusion between two people is to just talk.

The next morning, I sat in my study feeling as nervous as a young frogling again, wondering whether to take Fae's advice. "Oh, I just don't know... what if making the first move is not a good idea," I thought. Hesitantly, I picked up my mobile phone and stared at it for a while. Then, put it down and went to the kitchen to make a cup of tea.

"Yes or no?" I asked myself, staring out the window.
"Just talk!" Fae's words rang in my head.
"Okay, okay, I'll do it. And if I get no response from him, then I'll know for sure and I can stop fretting, right?" I made my tea and sat down with my phone again. "Now, yes, okay... here goes..." Slowly and carefully, I wrote a short, friendly text: "Hi, how are you? Hope you've recovered from the holidays." I pressed send, holding my breath but telling myself to expect nothing.

It took only a few seconds for my phone to beep with a reply. My heart skipped a beat as I excitedly read his reply. I responded immediately and before I knew it, we were having a conversation, exchanging several more messages. I found myself grinning inanely again. Afterwards, I laid my phone down and shed a few tears, feeling relieved, elated and a tiny bit annoyed at myself for getting so worked up over it all.

Once again, my amazing Fairy Godmother, this incredible, intuitive guidance system, had known better. Pete was indeed, different from all the rest. Apparently, he was rather shy and simply needed a little encouragement from me in order to feel reassured enough to make a move. I soon learned the steps of this new dance of communication that we had begun. I would take the first step and then, he would step forwards, responding with plenty of enthusiasm. Again, I was overwhelmed with love, happiness and gratitude for this extraordinary feeling growing between us.

As I got to know Pete, he slowly opened up about his past and I learned how this gentle, deeply caring man had also been hurt several times in his life. Hence, he had become wary of women, especially upon first encounters. After meeting me, he was afraid that I might be like all the rest, and would treat him like just another fleeting rainbow. Although we had spent much of our holiday together, he had assumed *I* was just having fun and he could not believe that this woman, from another country, could genuinely be interested in him. Now, it was my turn to show him that I would not give up and I was worth waiting for. With slow and persistent patience, honesty and kindness, his timidity fell away and was replaced with dependable consistency, trust and confidence.

Initially, I could hardly comprehend the magnitude of all that had happened. It was many months later that I began to accept that this was the real deal. It was like no one and nothing I had ever experienced before, a union that felt absolutely right, from the core of my being. Through every cell, physically, mentally and intrinsically, I knew that this was exactly what my heart had always been looking for. This was an unquestionable, genuine and authentic love; a connection with another human being on a much deeper level than I had ever experienced before. Since my early frogling years, I had always believed that this kind of connection was possible. It was a sense of knowing that, after all the challenges and journeys, I had finally, come home. I had grown, healed and come full circle and eventually, found a natural and peaceful relationship, one that was always meant to be.

You see, this was a union that had been made long, long ago in a different space and time, perhaps in another dimension, where we had agreed to be together. That is why we both felt so 'at home' with each other without even trying and why I had spent my whole life searching. It is the reason we matched so perfectly on just about every level, especially the *who* we were. Our souls recognised each other long before we had consciously met. They had connected by aligning our magical, creative thoughts to bring us together, in spite of the obstacles. Hence, when I wrote my perfect partner story, I innately knew what kind of man I needed. As with all things in nature, I simply had to connect to my true self and set my intention for our paths to cross. Thus, our destiny became synchronised and we both manifested a holiday; a time and place, where we could both meet.

Despite the miles apart, the princess and her new prince began to grow closer together. They found that when they connected, even on the telephone, they brought out the best of each other's frogginess and could spend hours just laughing and talking. Although she was unsure about the future, the princess felt completely happy and at peace knowing that whatever lay ahead, her fairy godmother was always beside her. Little did she know that her life had changed forever and there were yet many more adventures to take, magic to learn and a happy-ever-after to manifest.

The End...
...and a new beginning
* * *

About the Author

Nazish Shameem Qazi is of Bangladeshi heritage and grew up in England where she lived for most of her life. At age 31, she turned her life around, went back to university and discovered her true calling. In 2002, she graduated with an MSc in occupational psychology and since, has created a successful career in learning, training and personal development.

Her passion for transforming peoples' lives grew whilst working with the unemployed, drug and alcohol sufferers and young students. Along with designing and delivering training programs for business professionals, managers and CEOs, she has coached many to heal their hearts from emotional baggage, free their minds of self-doubt and go on to achieve personal and professional goals.

Nazish's teachings are backed by psychological knowledge as well as mental practices based on the Silva Method, NLP, neuroscience and other coaching techniques. She has also developed some powerful mind tools through working with her own clients and transforming their lives. As an author, business and life coach, her life-long intention has always been to help ordinary people realize their own extraordinary natures.

Nazish welcomes your thoughts, stories and ideas.
Contact her directly via:
Website: *www.jivondeesha.com*
Email: *lifepaths@jivondeesha.com*
Facebook: *Jivon-Deesha-Life-Paths*

Acknowledgements

First and foremost, it was my father who introduced me to the amazing abilities of our brains and the Silva Method. It was his continued interest in our potential as humans that awakened my passion and inevitably, led me to become a life coach. Thank you, Papa, for being an extraordinary human being and role model. I am forever grateful for your teachings that opened my mind, endless encouragement, and most of all, your immeasurable love.

Secondly, without my mother's blessings, support and wisdom, my career would undoubtedly never have taken off. Despite her personal reservations when I was young, she always backed my professional plans and guided my decision making. She inspired and influenced me in ways no-one else ever could. It was her staggering capacity to weather life's storms that gave me the strength to work through mine. It was the burden of her heartaches and sorrows that compelled me to write such a book. Thank you, Ammu, for being my unique, indomitable mother. I am who I am because of your abundant love, energy and joyful spirit.

Over the years, many, many friends, family, clients and even strangers have divulged their innermost secrets, shared their worries and opened their hearts to me. Most of them have graciously listened and accepted the ideas, suggestions and offerings that have come through my voice. For this beautiful gift and the opportunity to support and help, I am eternally grateful. In particular, I truly appreciate all of my dear clients whom I have had the privilege to coach. Without you all, I would not have been able to develop my unique 'mind-tools' – thank you.

I could probably write a whole chapter to express my heartfelt appreciation to all the potential partners who have come and gone in my life. My deepest thanks to you men for choosing me and for the experiences we had together. I am truly grateful for every happiness, hurdle and hardship that we shared. Without doubt, I would never have learned as much or understood the multi-faceted nature of human relationships, if you hadn't been a part of my life. Certainly, this book would not have come into being without you all. So, I thank you, sincerely and humbly, for loving, giving, teaching and testing me.

It was a particular conversation with my dearest friend, Vuyo, in September 2019, which firmly planted the seeds for writing this book. I am deeply grateful for your ideas about why the world needs to re-learn the secrets of awakening their self-knowledge, and for your exquisite words of wisdom about love, healing and energy. You have my heartfelt appreciation, dear soul sister, for your faith in me and your astounding ability to always tune-in, and of course, for challenging me to write this book – thank you!

Most of all, I have no words to describe my immense gratitude for having my *Mann* walk beside me and give me more than I ever imagined possible. His unwavering enthusiasm and encouragement have sprinkled the magic dust I needed to help this fairy tale take flight. I would never have imagined writing such fantastical truths if it weren't for his passion and expert advice, giving me courage in my art and writing. His own frogling story was also responsible for inspiring the concept behind the 'Frog Princess'. Thank you, my hero, for the beautiful cover design, technical know-how and for being my muse in writing this book. I am forever grateful for your consistent support in birthing my ideas and sharing every step of this journey with me.

Having applied my manifestation method at every step of this book's creation, I should not be surprised at the many 'coincidences' I have experienced along the way. Yet, I was amazed and utterly delighted to meet Daniella Blechner at a conference in January 2020. She turned out to be the perfect publisher for me, just as I had imagined and wished for. Finding the right publisher would otherwise, have been the hardest part of my book writing journey. So, a huge thank you Daniella, for going with your intuition and agreeing to publish and promote my book. I truly appreciate your patience, professionalism and most of all, your joyful exuberance about my work. I also want to praise and thank your proficient team at Conscious Dreams Publishing for all their hard work and in making this dream become a reality.

Finally, I thank YOU, dear reader, for taking the time to read, learn and grow. I truly hope, that by doing so, you will find your one, true love and manifest your own happy-ever-after. In any case, I am confident that by healing your heart and letting your love grow and spill over, you are doing good for many others, not only yourself. When your self-love deepens and you share that love with those around you, the ripples will spread wider than you might think. In so doing, you also help heal the world, for which, I applaud you and am incredibly grateful – thank you!

REFERENCES

Research, Notes and Suggested Reading

1. **Handwriting and drawing on paper:**
   Kiefer, M., Schuler, S., Mayer, C., Trumpp, N. M., Hille, K., & Sachse, S. (2015). Handwriting or Typewriting? The influence of pen- or keyboard-based writing training on reading and writing performance in preschool children. *Advances in Cognitive Psychology*, 11(4), 136–146.
   https://doi.org/10.5709/acp-0178-7

   Mueller, P. A., and Oppenheimer, D. M. (2014). The pen is mightier than the keyboard: advantages of longhand over laptop note taking. *Psychological Science*, 25(6), 1159–1168.
   https://doi.org/10.1177/0956797614524581

   Van der Meer, A., and Van der Weel, F. (2017). Only three fingers write, but the whole brain works: A high-density EEG study showing advantages of drawing over typing for learning. *Frontiers in Psychology*, 8, 706.
   https://doi.org/10.3389/fpsyg.2017.00706

2. **Psychology of falling in love:**
   Bartels, A., and Zeki, S. (2004). The neural correlates of maternal and romantic love. NeuroImage, 21(3), 1155–1166.
   https://doi.org/10.1016/j.neuroimage.2003.11.003

   Becker-Phelps, L., (2016). Love: *The Psychology of Attraction: A practical guide to successful dating and a happy relationship*. DK Publishing.

3. **Grief and loss:**
Kübler-Ross, E (1969). On Death and Dying. Retrieved from Gregory, C. *Five Stages of Grief,* Routledge.
https://www.psycom.net/depression.central.grief.html

Parkes, C. M. (1998). Bereavement in adult life. BMJ (Clinical research ed.), 316(7134), 856–859.
https://doi.org/10.1136/bmj.316.7134.856

Pass, O. M. (2006). Toni Morrison's Beloved: A journey through the pain of grief. *The Journal of Medical Humanities,* 27(2), 117-124.
https://doi.org/10.1007/s10912-006-9010-0

Suggested reading: Brown, B. (2015). *Rising Strong.* Penguin Random House.

4. **Stan and Ollie join the Foreign Legion:**
Sutherland A. E. (Director). (1939). *The Flying Deuces* [Film]. Boris Morros Productions.

5. **Silva BLS training course presented by John Newman in London, UK, 1983:**
Silva, J. (1960). The Silva Mind Control Method developed by Jose Silva. *The Silva Method.*
https://www.silvamethod.com/

6. **Relaxing meditation music:**
Higher Mind Royalty Free Music.
http://powerthoughtsmeditationclub.com/

7. **Gone With The Wind film:**
Fleming, V., Cukor, G. and Wood, S. (Directors). (1939). *Gone with the Wind* [Film]. Selznick International Picture.

8. **Mirror work:**
   Hay, L. (1991). *The Power is Within You.* Hay House Inc.

   Nichols, L. (2020). *Why Mirror Work Will Change Your Life.* [Film on Youtube].
   https://www.motivatingthemasses.com/mirror-work/

   Qazi, N. S. (2019). *Am I Happy with Myself? Turn fear into fuel and fire up your self-esteem.* Bookboon.com.
   https://bookboon.com/en/am-i-happy-with-myself-ebook

9. **Internal guidance system and Fae:**
   Gigerenzer, G. (2007). *Gut Feelings: Shortcuts to better decision making.* Penguin Books Ltd.

   Mulukom, V. (2018, May 16). Is it Rational to Trust Your Gut Feeling? A neuroscientist explains. *The Conversation*, UK.
   https://theconversation.com/is-it-rational-to-trust-your-gut-feelings-a-neuroscientist-explains-95086

   Newton, M. (1994). *Journey of Souls: Case Studies of Life Between Lives.* Llewellyn Publications.

10. **Alpha level brain wave frequency:**
    Berger, H (1929). Über das Elektrenkephalogramm des Menschen. *Archiv für Psychiatrie und Nervenkrankheiten* (in German). 87 (1): 527–570. doi: 10.1007/BF01797193.

    Kotsos, T. (2021, Jan.). Brain Waves and the Deeper States of Consciousness. *Mind Your Reality.*
    https://www.mind-your-reality.com/brain_waves.html

11. **Subconscious or unconscious mind:**
    Ritter, S., Barren, R. B. and Dijksterhuis, A. (2012). Creativity: The Role of Unconscious Processes in Idea Generation and Idea Selection. *Thinking Skills and Creativity.* 7. 21–27. DOI: 10.1016/j.tsc.2011.12.002

    Tracey, B. The role your subconscious mind plays on your everyday life. *Brian Tracy International.*
    https://www.briantracy.com/blog/personal-success/subconscious-mind-everyday-life/

    Williams, R. Processing Information with Nonconscious Mind. *Journal Psyche.*
    http://journalpsyche.org/processing-information-with-nonconscious-mind/

12. **Visual, auditory and kinaesthetic styles:**
    Barsch, J. (1980). Barsch Learning Style Inventory. *Semantics Scholar.*
    https://sarconline.sdes.ucf.edu/wp-content/uploads/sites/19/2017/07/Barsch_Learning_Styles_Inventory11.pdf

    Visual Learners Convert Words to Pictures in the Brain and Vice Versa, Says Psychology Study. (2009, March 28). *ScienceDaily.*
    www.sciencedaily.com/releases/2009/03/090325091834.htm

13. **Developing fears and beliefs in childhood:**
    Lipton, B. (2015) *The Biology of Belief: Unleashing the Power of Consciousness*, Matter and Miracles. Hay House Publishers.

14. **Carl Jung's theory of the shadow self:**
    Johnson, R. A. (1991). *Owning Your Own Shadow: Understanding the dark side of the Psyche.* Harper Collins Publishers.

15. **Recognising patterns and programmes:**
    Qazi, N. S. (2018). Am I Happy with Others? Reinvent Difficult Work Relationships. *Bookboon.*
    https://bookboon.com/en/am-i-happy-with-others-ebook

16. **Definition of the word 'forgive': Collinsdictionary.com:**
    https://www.collinsdictionary.com/dictionary/english/forgive

17. **The conscious and subconscious:**
    Freud's Model of the Human Mind. (2018). *Journal Psyche.*
    http://journalpsyche.org/understanding-the-human-mind/#more-169

18. **The Reticular Activation System:**
    Hendry, R., and Crippen, D. (2014). *ACS Surgery: Principles and practice critical care.* DOI: 10.2310/7800.2159.

19. **Can the brain tell the difference between reality and imagination?**
    Hamilton, D. R. (2014, Oct 30). Does your brain distinguish real from imaginary? *Dr David R. Hamilton.*
    https://drdavidhamilton.com/does-your-brain-distinguish-real-from-imaginary/

    Murphy, J. (2007). *The Power of Your Subconscious Mind.* Wilder Publications.

20. **Wayne Dyer quote:**
    Medrut, F. (2018, Mar 29) 20 Wayne Dyer quotes on manifesting your destiny. *Goal Cast.*
    https://www.goalcast.com/2018/03/29/20-wayne-dyer-quotes/

21. Changing your vibration:

Choquette, S. (1997). *Your Heart's Desire: Instructions for Creating the Life You Really Want.* Hay House UK.

Hicks, E. and Hicks, J. (2013). *The Essential Law of Attraction Collection.* Hay House Inc.

22. Emotional frequencies:

Eijlers, E., Smidts, A. and Boksem, M. A. S. (2019). Implicit measurement of emotional experience and its dynamics. *PLOS ONE*, 14(2): e0211496.
https://doi.org/10.1371/journal.pone.0211496

Song, L. Z., Schwartz, G. E. and Russek, L. G. (1998). Heart-focused attention and heart-brain synchronization: energetic and physiological mechanisms. *Alternative therapies in health and medicine*, 4(5), 44-62.

23. Creating coherence between mind and emotion:

Dispenza, J. (2017). *Becoming Supernatural: How common people are doing the uncommon.* Hay House Inc.

24. Heart-brain coherence:

Childre, D., Martin, H., Rozman, D. and McCraty, R. (2016). *Heart Intelligence: Connecting with the Intuitive Guidance of the Heart.* Waterfront Press

McCraty, Rollin. (2003). The Energetic Heart: Biolectromagnetic Interactions Within and Between People. *The Neuropsychotherapist*. 6. 22-43. DO – 10.12744/tnpt(6)022-043

Conscious Dreams
PUBLISHING

Be the author of your own destiny

www.consciousdreamspublishing.com

info@consciousdreamspublishing.com

Let's connect